DOING GOOD
FOR THE AGED

Volunteers in an Ombudsman Program

Pat M. Keith

PRAEGER

Westport, Connecticut
London

Library of Congress Cataloging-in-Publication Data

Keith, Pat M.
  Doing good for the aged : volunteers in an ombudsman program / Pat M. Keith
    p. cm.
  Includes bibliographical references and index.
  ISBN 0–275–97698–X (alk. paper)
    1. Aged volunteers—United States. 2. Voluntarism—United States. I. Title.
HN90.V64 K43   2003
361.3'7—dc21   2002028313

British Library Cataloguing in Publication Data is available.

Library of Congress Catalog Card Number: 2002028313
ISBN: 0–275–97698–X

First published in 2003

Praeger Publishers, 88 Post Road West, Westport, CT 06881
An imprint of Greenwood Publishing Group, Inc.
www.praeger.com

Printed in the United States of America

The paper used in this book complies with the
Permanent Paper Standard issued by the National
Information Standards Organization (Z39.48–1984).

10 9 8 7 6 5 4 3 2 1

For Inez and Arthur, who both cared

"A care facility should not be a punishment for having lived so long."
—*Resident Advocate*

"We don't have much to look forward to here but mealtimes, so why can't they be a more pleasant experience?"
—*Resident Advocate*

"Again, all aspects were very positive. Good food, care excellent, clean facility, no odors, residents happy."
—*Committee Report*

"My greatest difficulties are with residents who fear retribution and are afraid to report anything."
—*Resident Advocate*

"When thou liest down, thou shalt not be afraid ... and thy sleep shall be sweet."
—*Proverbs 3:24*

Contents

Tables

Acknowledgments

I am grateful to personnel at the Iowa Department of Elder Affairs, without whose help and hospitality I would never have been able to conduct this research. I express my thanks to Kris Bullington (state resident advocate committee coordinator), Carl McPherson (former state long-term care ombudsman), and Debi Meyers (interim state long-term care ombudsman) for providing access to information, answering a myriad of questions, expressing encouragement, and perhaps above all, letting my colleagues and me be "under foot" many days as we coded.

Much appreciation goes to coordinators of resident advocate committees at the Area Agencies on Aging for their assistance and use of their records. Thanks to them and their directors for permitting the intrusion and welcoming us.

My colleague LaDonna Osborn deserves much credit for her fine secretarial assistance, her insights, and her enormous patience. The book would not have been completed without her help. Thanks to Renea Miller for applying her computer skills in designing the questionnaire.

I appreciate more than I can say the support of the AARP Andrus Foundation. Their patience and time extensions permitted me to complete the research with some additional features. This activity has meant a lot to me.

Finally, to the 778 volunteers who shared so much, I say "Thanks!" Some of your words will long remain in my mind and heart. As the literature suggests, your job is not an easy one!

Chapter 1

Introduction

Early in their work on older volunteers, Fischer and Schaffer (1993) observed that voluntarism as a field of research was relatively new and quite limited. A little later, however, an entire chapter on volunteering was included in an encyclopedia of current research and thought about aging (Harootyan, 1996). Research on volunteering by older persons is no longer peripheral to the field of aging. This book is about the subjective and objective outcomes of the work of volunteer advocates in nursing facilities. The majority of the volunteers sampled were older, and they served older persons through their work in an ombudsman program.

There is now a significant body of literature on volunteerism and about older volunteers in particular (Bull & Levine, 1993; Cnaan, Handy, & Wadsworth, 1996; Fischer & Schaffer, 1993; Goss, 1999; Harootyan, 1996; Midlarsky & Kahana, 1994; Musick, Herzog, & House, 1999; Oman, Thoresen, & McMahon, 1999; Scott & Caldwell, 1996; Stebbins, 1996; Van Willigen, 2000; Young & Glasgow, 1998; Zweigenhaft, Armstrong, Quintis, & Riddick, 1996). Many of the efforts of older volunteers are devoted to helping other older persons. In this book, *volunteer work* refers to unpaid work on behalf of others with the objective of benefiting them. Furthermore, volunteer work is defined as unpaid work to assist others with whom individuals have no familial or other obligatory ties. Volunteers, however, are not precluded from benefiting from their work. In contrast to informal caregiving, volunteering is more formal and public (Wilson, 2000).

The extent of involvement of older persons in volunteering suggests its importance. A high percentage of older persons volunteer, a significant proportion of volunteers are older persons, volunteer efforts of some elders comprise a substantial portion of their activities, and older persons disproportionately volunteer in capacities in which they serve other elders (Caro & Bass, 1995; Fischer

& Schaffer, 1993; Van Willigen, 2000). The significance of contributions through volunteering by older persons, and the extent to which they account for increments in volunteering in the last few decades, especially that of women over age 60, was noted by Goss (1999).

Volunteering is an important area of study in the field of aging because it increasingly sustains human service programs for both the young and old, because it provides meaningful activities that continue to integrate older persons into the larger society, and because it may empower both volunteers and the recipients of their efforts. Indeed, a meta-analysis of thirty-seven separate studies concluded that volunteering brought about positive change among both older volunteers and those whom they served and that the former were a significant resource to meet service needs of vulnerable groups of various ages (Wheeler, Gorey, & Greenblatt, 1998). Because of the work of older volunteers, current services of social welfare and health agencies, churches, and civic organizations are maintained and expansion of their services is possible (Okun, Barr, & Herzog, 1998). In addition to the assistance provided to organized services, many personal benefits of volunteering for participants have been documented, ranging from feelings of competency and self-esteem (Herzog, Franks, Markus, & Holmberg, 1998) to increased life satisfaction (Van Willigen, 2000) to reduced mortality (Oman et al., 1999).

In research about older volunteers, considerable attention has been given to their demographic characteristics. There are some relatively consistent findings, although the relationships between demographic characteristics of older volunteers and the magnitude of participation are not always direct. Higher rates of volunteerism are often associated with higher education, income, occupational status, employment (especially part-time), and good health (Bull & Levine, 1993; Fischer & Schaffer, 1993; Van Willigen, 2000). The relationship between gender, marital status, race, religion, region, and volunteering is sometimes less direct (Bull & Levine, 1993; Fischer & Schaffer, 1993; Wilson, 2000).

The settings in which older persons volunteer vary considerably. Characteristics of the organizations in which volunteers assist may affect outcomes of their efforts, both for themselves and the recipients of their help. The type of organization or program, its size, location (rural, urban), age of a program or organization, and kind of volunteer activity have been studied (Fischer & Schaffer, 1993; Independent Sector, 1998).

The range of volunteer activities and the skills they demand are marked. For example, taking tickets at an event, distributing leaflets, assisting at a bake sale, and serving as a resident advocate are all opportunities for volunteering in which older persons may participate. The context in which advocacy occurs and the activities that are expected are quite differentiated from some other forms of volunteering. Advocates may confront issues that encompass the "entire spectrum of problems plaguing America's long-term care residents, from rape to wrongful death to cold food" (Nelson, 1995, p. 28). This indicates the importance, range, and magnitude of the tasks that volunteer advocates may encounter.

THE CONTEXT OF RESEARCH ON ADVOCACY IN NURSING FACILITIES

The legislative context of nursing home reform, including the amended Older Americans Act, requiring states to establish nursing home ombudsman/advocacy programs, has been described elsewhere (Filinson, 1995; Harris-Wehling, Feasley, & Estes, 1995; Huber, Borders, Netting, & Kautz, 2000; Netting, Huber, Paton, & Kautz, 1995). The office of the ombudsman is to "investigate and resolve complaints made by long-term care residents [and] monitor laws, regulations, and policies affecting long-term care" (Netting & Hinds, 1984, p. 13).

The health, safety, welfare, and rights of residents in long-term care facilities are the focus of the tasks of volunteer advocates. The ombudsman program was a product of the 1970s, "a decade of heightened and zealous concerns with patients' rights" (Monk, Kaye, & Litwin, 1984, p. 8). The program was to increase accountability of long-term care services: "Ordinary regulatory mechanisms do not work with services which have disabled, powerless people as their clientele" (9).

Provision of training for volunteers and promotion of citizen participation in the ombudsman program are a part of the mandate. The establishment of a community presence in long-term facilities, in large part, is formally accomplished by volunteers. Indeed, volunteers are linchpins in the community presence in long-term care facilities, although views of volunteers in ombudsman programs are infrequently studied.

Integration of members of the community into long-term care facilities may increase opportunities for residents, staff, and members of the community to socialize and to interact with one another. The thinking is that the presence of members of the community in long-term care facilities will have a positive effect on both residents and staff. Tourigny-Rivard and Drury (1987), for example, observed that even depressed residents benefited from the presence of volunteers. The integration of the community into long-term care facilities may affect how staff view their work and encourage them to provide higher-quality care, help them to understand the needs of residents, and enhance their well-being.

Ombudsman programs are based on the assumption that community involvement will have a "watchdog" effect on behalf of residents and increase accountability among staff and administrators of nursing homes (Monk et al., 1984). Such accountability may be attained informally or at the other extreme, by litigation.

The potential tension in such situations has contributed to views of the tasks of volunteers in ombudsman programs as stressful. "The work of the ombudsman is the most difficult in the field of Aging" (Monk et al., 1984, p. 165). "[A]s volunteer jobs go, the ombudsman job is a tough one" (Nelson, 1995, p. 27). I assumed that some of the difficulties and stressful aspects of advocacy would apply to the experiences and efforts of the volunteers who were studied in this research.

The nature of the activities performed by volunteers, including advocates, may affect their recruitment. Recruitment of volunteers is a widely recognized challenge in the administration of most volunteer programs. Preferred types of participation vary among older and younger volunteers, who contribute time to different kinds of organizations. Consequently, age differences in preferences for work will affect recruitment of volunteers. Younger persons volunteer in organizations that are extensions of their other roles, such as in work and child care. School-related volunteering is a frequent choice of younger volunteers (Wilson & Musick, 1997). In contrast, only 22 percent of older persons volunteer in educational organizations (Independent Sector, 1998), and they are less often participants in political organizations (Sundeen, 1990). But as many as 65 percent of older people contribute time to religious groups (Independent Sector, 1998).

Schiman and Lordeman (1989) concluded that assistance with recruitment is the most important need in long-term care ombudsman programs. Recruitment of volunteers to work in a long-term setting may be especially difficult. Perry's (1983) investigation of nonvolunteers' preferences for types of volunteer activities indicated that involvement in nursing homes was an infrequent choice of potential volunteers. Only 6 percent expressed interest in volunteering in a nursing home.

Little research has been done on the reasons persons volunteer to work in ombudsman programs, although there is considerable inquiry on motivations of volunteers in general (Wilson, 2000). Clary, Snyder, and Stukas (1996) asked why some persons choose to engage in unpaid work as volunteers. Much of the fascination with this question may be because "people participate in volunteer work in the face of substantial obstacles—it is effortful, it is work and work performed on an unpaid basis, it is time consuming, and it involves interactions with strangers" (Clary et al., 1996, p. 485). In fact, some volunteering is very difficult and trying.

One group of theories that attempts to explain volunteering through the use of individual attributes emphasizes motives or self-understandings, whereas others focus on rational action and cost-benefit analysis (Wilson, 2000). To explain why persons volunteer, scholars have developed several categories of reasons or motivations for participation. Following a functionalist approach, Clary et al. (1996) considered multiple motivations for volunteering that help individuals attain important psychological goals. Volunteering may satisfy six functions: values, understanding, enhancement, career, social, and protective (Clary et al., 1996). Persons will attempt to satisfy varied motivations through volunteering. Similar activities may be used to address different goals. From the literature, Fischer and Schaffer (1993) derived eight categories of motivations for volunteering: altruistic, ideological, egoistic, material reward, status/reward, social relationship, leisure time, and personal growth, along with multiple motivations. When asked why they volunteer, a majority of volunteers revealed altruistic motivations such as "wanting to help, wanting to be useful, having a sense of social responsibility, or wanting to do good" (Fischer & Schaffer, 1993, p. 43).

Nathanson and Eggleton's (1993) study of motivations for volunteering among fifty-three active and fifty-three inactive ombudsmen illustrates how reasons may be specific to a particular type of activity while at the same time, others may reflect motivations applicable to any volunteer tasks. The largest percentage of ombudsmen mentioned advocacy as a reason for volunteering (38 percent); others noted giving to the community (28 percent) and having had family in a nursing home (20 percent) as motivations for their involvement. The least often mentioned reasons were to obtain job experience or to fulfill an educational requirement (7 percent) and empathy for the aged (5 percent). There was no association between age, gender, and whether volunteers were active or inactive. Furthermore, those whose motivation was advocacy for the elderly were most likely to have volunteered at least one year. Chapter 3 presents some of the demographic correlates of interests and skills of volunteers who are described in this book.

ORIENTATIONS OF VOLUNTEERS IN OMBUDSMAN PROGRAMS

A portion of previous research on advocates has focused on volunteers' orientations to their roles and perceptions of their performance (Monk et al., 1984; Nelson, 1995). Volunteers have differing orientations to their work in ombudsman programs. Orientations of volunteers may include those of advocate, therapeutic supporter (friendly visitor), mediator, and educator (Harris-Wehling et al., 1995; Monk et al., 1984). Activities of the first three types have been studied most frequently.

Volunteers who identify as advocates may take partisan positions. In this type of orientation, the individual takes sides, acts as an advocate, and may engage in confrontations. This role is more active than the other orientations, and it reflects a results-oriented perspective (Monk et al., 1984). Another role is that of mediator, who is impartial, independent, nonpartisan, and nonjudgmental.

A third orientation toward the role of ombudsman is described as "therapeutically supportive." In this capacity, individual action centers on emotional support and friendly concern or caring (Monk et al., 1984). Some volunteers with this orientation may serve primarily as friendly visitors. Volunteers more often describe themselves as friendly visitors than as advocates or mediators (Monk et al., 1984).

A fourth type of orientation or approach, that of educator, has been considered (National Center for State Long-Term Care Ombudsman Resources, 1992). In this role, an ombudsman may educate residents, families, staff of facilities, and others about residents' rights. This book uses the three orientations on which Monk et al. (1984) conducted considerable research. The concerns of these three orientations—the mediator, the advocate, and the therapeutic supporter—overlap somewhat and are not mutually exclusive. In the present research, volunteers noted which of the three orientations with which they primarily identified. Correlates of and the significance of orientations of volunteers are considered in chapters 6 and 7. The variation in volunteers' conceptions of their roles in ombudsman programs, their attributions to administrators and others who work with residents, and the implications of the attitudes for volunteers are described more fully in chapter 8.

EFFECTIVENESS OF OMBUDSMEN

Some research has examined the effectiveness of ombudsman programs (Cherry, 1991; Nelson, Huber, & Walter, 1995). In general, these studies do not focus specifically on volunteers or link assessments of their participation with outcomes of their efforts, even though much of the work in ombudsman programs has been undertaken by these laypersons. Some research suggests that efforts of volunteers may be effective. In fact, nationally, employment of volunteers in ombudsman programs was found to be associated with a higher rate of resolution of complaints (Department of Health and Human Services, Office of the Inspector General, 1991). Self-assessments of one sample of volunteers confirmed views of their effectiveness. For example, volunteers observed that for the most part, their influence on long-term care was positive (Nelson, 1995).

At the time he conducted a study in Missouri, Cherry (1991) found that 32 percent of the nursing homes had volunteer ombudsman programs. Facilities with ombudsmen also were more likely to have other types of volunteer programs (52 percent) in which individuals participated in on-site musical, religious, or visitation activities. Availability of ombudsman programs was the most important factor that contributed to better-quality care in intermediate-care facilities but not in skilled nursing facilities. Rather, the presence of ombudsman programs was associated with higher-quality care in skilled nursing homes in which staffing of registered nurses also was ample (Cherry, 1991). Other volunteer programs alone did not affect the quality of care.

Nelson, Huber, and Walter (1995) observed that reporting of abuse, which is required by statute, was disproportionately greater in Oregon facilities with ombudsmen. In addition, ombudsmen were instrumental in attaining increased letters of reprimand and a greater number of identified deficiencies. Nelson and colleagues concluded that their research provided strong evidence that the presence of an ombudsman does make a difference.

Litwin and Monk (1987, p. 102) contend that nursing home ombudsmen make a difference in the "significant aspects of day to day life in long-term care facilities" by calling "attention to those aspects of quality of care that are not currently assured by other protective mechanisms." Through efforts of ombudsmen, facilities are encouraged to provide more than a minimum level of care.

Netting and Hinds (1989, p. 421) note that there has been little "attempt to address the advantages and difficulties encountered in implementing the program [ombudsman] in predominately rural communities." Yet there are reasons to consider rural and urban differences in ombudsman services. For example, in other types of programs that rely on volunteers, the number of unserved referrals are greater in projects in rural areas (Lee & Gray, 1992). Netting and Hinds (1989) observe that even in urban areas where long-term care facilities are perhaps somewhat more accessible and recruitment, retention, and coordination may be managed in greater proximity, there are difficulties in implementing programs. In rural areas, distance between communities and varied availability of services may further complicate these functions. On the other hand, the ombudsman program that is administered from an urban area may help connect residents of rural counties to extracommunity organizations. Characteristics of volunteers and of facilities, community size, number of complaints and resolutions, and orientations toward advocacy of volunteers in both rural and urban areas are investigated in later chapters.

OUTLINE OF THE BOOK

Chapter 2 contains descriptions of the procedures for sample selection and sources of data used in this book. The sample of volunteers, the mail questionnaire and its contents, information about the number and nature of complaints filed, and data available from the application form are introduced.

"Pathways to Volunteering," chapter 3, considers interests that figured in volunteers' decisions to become involved in the ombudsman program. Skills volunteers believe they bring to their work are less often studied than their reasons for participation or factors that prompt their involvement. In chapter 3, interests and skills of volunteers are investigated in relation to demographic characteristics (age, education, gender, employment status, and earlier volunteer experiences).

The application form filed prior to becoming a volunteer comprises time 1 data that are compared with participants' later views of the volunteer experience. In chapter 4, for example, anticipated difficulties are compared with those actually realized by volunteers later in their work. Discrepancies between what volunteers believed their work would be like and events that actually happened are important to assist future participants in avoiding difficulties or instances of unpreparedness and for those who train volunteers.

In chapter 5, several social-psychological indicators of volunteers' observations about their work are examined in relation to their demographic characteristics, training and education experiences, and aspects of participation. The intent of the chapter is to determine which, if any, of these personal character-istics, training and education, or characteristics of participation predict social-psychological outcomes of the volunteer experience.

Chapter 6 contains an analysis of correlates of volunteers' orientations to their work. The relative importance of demographic characteristics, in-service training, inequity, and hindrances in differentiating among the primary role orientations of advocate, mediator, therapeutic supporter, and a mixed pattern are studied.

Needs for care by elders vary in rural and urban communities. Analyses in chapter 7 suggest that size of community, volunteer role orientations, and ac-quaintance with nursing facility staff may jointly influence the number of complaints filed by volunteers and therefore, the investigative process.

Literature suggests that relationships between volunteers and nursing facil-ity staff may be quite variable depending on the role orientations of the former. Analyses in chapter 8 consider how role orientations of volunteers are differ-entiated by their attributions to nursing facility personnel, perceived effective-ness, and the number of unresolved complaints.

Several sources of support and their importance to volunteers make up a por-tion of chapter 9. These sources range from fellow participants to facility staff and residents to persons outside the nursing home. Selected types of support figured in the efficacy of volunteers.

Training and educational activities for volunteers benefit both them and the organizations they serve. Chapter 10 shows how training and education activi-ties and assessments of those activities affected feelings of efficacy and worry among volunteers in the ombudsman program.

Chapter 11 contains descriptions of benefits, advice, and recommendations by current participants for future volunteers. In chapter 12, I summarize the findings with attention to implications for practice.

Chapter 2

Procedures and Characteristics of the Sample

SAMPLE SELECTION PROCEDURES

The objective of this research was to obtain information on the work and outcomes of participation of persons who volunteered to serve on resident advocate committees in nursing facilities in Iowa. The population of interest comprised all individuals who were currently serving on volunteer resident advocate committees in each of the nursing facilities located in eight Area Agencies on Aging in Iowa. The volunteers were not certified ombudsmen but were volunteer resident advocates in an ombudsman program.

The sampling frame was a list of all committee members in each nursing facility located in eight Area Agencies on Aging. This list, provided by the Department of Elder Affairs, was given to the Iowa State University Statistical Laboratory along with a list of nursing facilities and the size of their resident advocate committees. There were 1,808 committee members distributed throughout 320 care facilities. Preliminary analyses indicated that the sizes of the committees ranged between one and fourteen members, with the majority of committees (80 percent) having between four and eight members.

Resources were available to survey one thousand committee members. A two-stage cluster design was used, in which the cluster (first-stage sample unit) is a nursing facility resident advocate committee and the element within the cluster (second-stage sample unit) is a committee member. Because of the small number of nursing home facilities in relation to the total sample size, each facility was included in the sample with certainty.

Volunteers were sampled from each resident advocate committee with equal probability within the committee. The sample size of one thousand was allocated roughly in proportion to the committee size to generate a sample that would be approximately self-weighting. Deviations from proportional allocation were implemented to ensure that an adequate number of volunteers were sampled from small committees and to place a cap on the number of members selected from the largest committees.

The following selection algorithm was used to determine the number of members to be sampled in each resident advocate committee:

- If a committee had two or fewer members, all members were included in the sample with certainty.
- If a committee had three members, two members were selected for the sample with equal probability.
- If a committee had nine or more members, five members were selected from the committee with equal probability.

Once the sample allocation had been determined for the small (three or fewer) and larger (ten or greater) committees, the remaining sample size was calculated. The remainder of the sample was allocated across the 256 committees with four to eight members in proportion to the committee size (i.e., fewer members were sampled in smaller committees relative to the sample size for larger committees within this range). A cumulate and round procedure was used to generate integer sample sizes using this rule. Within each committee with three or more volunteers, an independent systematic sample was selected. This procedure resulted in a sample size of 999 volunteers.

Much of the data in this book were analyzed from responses of 778 volunteers to a mail questionnaire. There was a 78 percent rate of return. Reasons for nonresponse were sometimes attributable to illness or, more rarely, death, unwillingness to participate, incomplete questionnaires, completion of the same questionnaire by multiple members of a committee, and resignation from the program between the time the list of members was produced and volunteers were contacted.

TYPES OF DATA COLLECTION

In this section, I describe the three types of data collection employed in the research. Data collection included a mail questionnaire sent to volunteers, an application form completed for the state Department of Elder Affairs by persons who later became volunteers, and information about complaints filed on behalf of nursing home residents and from records retained at the Area Agencies on Aging.

The Mail Questionnaire

Structured Questions

The mail questionnaire contained both structured and unstructured questions. The majority of the questions in the questionnaire were structured.

Structured questions that have fixed responses, such as "Strongly agree" to "Strongly disagree," were often summed to form scales. Some of the scales were drawn from the work of Monk et al. (1984). Scales from structured questions were compiled to assess views of volunteers in several areas, including the following: importance of areas of work of advocates; job satisfaction; role strain (including perceptions of equity, turnover, training, responsibility, worry, and fellow volunteers); hindrances; views of the work of advocates by facility administrators, care facility staff, and others; efficacy; effectiveness in specific areas; support received; and support needed. Scale items and descriptive statistics about them are presented when the scales are discussed in the text.

Unstructured Questions

Unstructured or open-response questions are those with no predetermined categories for a respondent to check. In addition to replying to scale items and questions requiring structured answers, respondents described more about their work as volunteers in answer to the ten unstructured questions. All questions about volunteers and volunteering refer to resident advocate volunteers. The following unstructured questions were asked:

1. What are some of the positive things about being a resident advocate volunteer?
2. If you could give advice to others who are or may become volunteers, what would your advice be?
3. Did you receive formal orientation training through a workshop or some other method for your duties as a volunteer? Describe.
4. Have you received additional formal training for your volunteer tasks beyond your initial orientation training? Describe.
5. What recommendations do you have for training new volunteers?
6. Based on your experience, what are the major reasons resident advocate volunteers leave?
7. Has being a volunteer changed your view of long-term care facilities? Describe.
8. Has being a volunteer changed the way you think about old age? Describe.
9. If you had it to do over again, would you become a resident advocate volunteer? Describe.
10. What is the hardest thing about being a resident advocate volunteer?

The principal investigator and a student separately reviewed answers to the ten questions and developed multiple categories for each. This procedure permitted a cross check of decisions of two independent reviewers about the development and use of the categories. Each category was assigned a number or a code. Using the categories, responses of each of the 778 volunteers to the ten questions were coded. The response categories developed for each question are presented in the chapters in which they are analyzed.

Data from Application Forms

Persons who want to serve as volunteers complete application forms that are retained at the Department of Elder Affairs. In this research, the applications resident advocates filed before their selection constitute "pre"-data in a number of areas. Data were coded from several questions by a colleague and the author at the Department of Elder Affairs.

Responses to some questions were short paragraphs or brief essays that were mostly handwritten. It was necessary to read these answers and code them into standardized categories. The same procedure used with open-response questions in the mail questionnaire was employed to develop categories for unstructured questions in the application form and to code them.

The following information was coded from the application forms:

1. Age.
2. Sex.
3. Occupational status.
4. Previous occupational status.
5. Reasons for interest in becoming a resident advocate committee member (the first reasons were analyzed here).
6. How the applicant became aware of resident advocate committees.
7. How volunteers believed they could help residents.
8. Volunteers' past and present work experiences that may relate to resident advocate activities.
9. Volunteers' past and present volunteer experiences that may relate to resident advocate activities. The following categories were used: service and fraternal organizations, recreational groups, political and civic groups, job-related organizations, church-related groups, youth groups, and groups for the aged.
10. Skills applicants believe they have that would be useful on a resident advocate committee.
11. Most difficult aspect of being a resident advocate volunteer.
12. Familiarity and contact with facilities (coded "yes" or "no").

    a. Own or have a financial interest in a facility/facilities.
    b. Consult professionally with a facility/facilities.
    c. Work in a facility/facilities.
    d. Employed at some time by a facility.
    e. Related to (an) employee(s) of a facility.
    f. A member of the board of directors of a facility/facilities.
    g. A public employee who sponsors or places residents in facilities.
    h. Inspect or evaluate facilities professionally.

i. Administer a facility/facilities.

j. Know people well who work for the facility for which I am applying.

k. Know people who live in the facility for which I am applying.

l. Related to (an) owner/licensee of a facility.

Data for respondents from the application form were linked with those from the questionnaire.

Committee Data

Data about the type and number of complaints filed by respondents were coded on site at the eight Area Agencies on Aging. Information was obtained from committee minutes and from quarterly forms that were filed. The following data related to committees, and their working environment were coded:

1. Total number of complaints by type (resident care, physician services, medications, financial, food/nutrition, administrative, resident rights, building sanitation, laundry, actions of reimbursement agencies, actions of regulatory agencies, and actions of others).

2. Total number of complaints.

3. Total number of resolutions of complaints.

4. Number of resolutions by volunteers.

5. Number of resolutions by others.

6. Number of complaints referred to Department of Elder Affairs.

7. Number of complaints referred to other agencies.

8. Total number of reports of volunteer activities available.

9. Size of facility (actual size coded).

10. Number on the committee.

11. Number of committee members chosen in the sample.

12. Number of respondents per committee.

13. Facility type (1 = profit; 2 = nonprofit).

14. Population size of the city in which the facility was located (see chapter 7 for the code).

Data from the questionnaires, application forms, and reports of complaints were linked in a single file. This made it possible to consider relationships among persons' assessments reported on the questionnaire, data on their work as committee members, and their views noted on the application prior to becoming a volunteer. Sample size varies some across the chapters because subsamples used in the analyses differ.

CHARACTERISTICS OF THE SAMPLE

Personal Characteristics of Volunteers

Volunteers who responded to the questionnaire ranged from 32 to 91 years of age ($\bar{X}$ = 69; median = 71; sd = 10.14). Seventy-six percent were women; 65 percent of the sample were married, 28 percent were widowed, 4 percent were divorced or separated, and 4 percent never married. Men were a larger proportion of nonrespondents (34 percent) than they were of the group of respondents. Men were also younger than the mean age of the total sample ($\bar{X}$ = 65 years).

Compared with some other samples of older persons, these volunteers had considerable formal education. Six percent had attended only elementary school; 36 percent graduated from high school, 31 percent had completed some college or had finished a two-year degree, 11 percent had a four-year degree, and 16 percent had undertaken graduate work.

The sample had very positive ratings of health. Almost one-quarter rated their health as excellent, and 61 percent enjoyed good health. Fourteen percent had fair health, with less than 2 percent reporting poor or very poor physical health.

At the time of their application, 55 percent of the volunteers were retired, and another 17 percent listed homemaker as their current occupation. The retired and homemakers constituted the two largest groups of applicants.

If applicants were retired, they were asked about their occupation prior to retirement. The occupational groups in which the most retired volunteers had been employed were: professions (22 percent), clerical or sales (19 percent), administrative (10 percent), farm operators (8 percent), and service workers (6 percent). Because of their large numbers and training related to volunteer activities, nurses and aids were coded separately from the professional group. Thirteen percent had worked as nurses, and another 6 percent had been employed in nursing homes. About 3 percent had been employed in each of the following occupational groups: skilled craftsmen, foremen, and business owners. Fewer than 3 percent listed homemaking as a former occupation.

When they applied, 5 percent were still employed in either clerical, sales, or administrative positions, 4 percent were in the clergy, and 2 to 3 percent of the applicants were service workers, business owners, or nurses. Any remaining occupational classifications included fewer than 2 percent of the applicants.

After they became volunteers and when they completed the mail questionnaire, 10 percent were employed full-time and 15 percent worked part-time, 16 percent were homemakers, and 54 percent were retired. Three percent were placed in an "other" category, which included students and those who identified themselves as disabled. A little over 1 percent described themselves as unemployed.

The slight differences observed between the application and questionnaire data in the percentages of volunteers who were retired and homemakers were likely due to shifts in employment in the interval between the two contacts.

Yearly gross household income was coded into eight categories ranging from less than $5,000 (1) to $75,000 and over (8). The mean, median, and modal income category was $25,000–$34,999, with 25 percent of the sample in this group (sd = 1.64). Forty percent had incomes below $25,000. Another quarter had annual incomes between $35,000 and $59,999, and 10 percent received $60,000 or above. About one-fifth did not report their income. Consequently, income is not used in any of the multivariate analyses.

Characteristics of Participation

The size of committees in which responding volunteers worked ranged from one to thirteen members ($\bar{X}$ = 5.78; median = 5; sd = 2.14). Facilities ranged in size from 20 to 717 residents ($\bar{X}$ = 80; median = 68; sd = 52.27).

Volunteers on committees served as either chair, secretary, or a member. Of the sample, 19 percent were chairs, 14 percent secretaries, and 66 percent were committee members who did not hold office at the time of the research.

Volunteers' length of service ranged from less than six months to twenty-seven years, with a mean of six years ($\bar{X}$ = 6.3 years; median = 5 years; sd = 4.86). The number of hours volunteers spent on advocacy activities per month ranged from one to forty-seven hours ($\bar{X}$ = 6 hours; median = 4 hours; sd = 6.12).

Volunteers indicated how often they had contact with each resident. Codes were assigned to categories of contact for use in later analysis. Contact with residents ranged from less than once a year (coded "1"; 1.7 percent); one time per year (coded "2"; 10 percent); two times per year to quarterly (coded "3"; 39 percent); more than quarterly but less than monthly (coded "4"; 13.1 percent); monthly or more often, but not weekly (coded "5"; 27.1 percent); or weekly (coded "6"; 9.1 percent, $\bar{X}$ = 3.81; median = 3.00; sd = 1.25). To summarize, the largest proportion of volunteers contacted residents two to four times per year (39 percent), but 36 percent met with residents in their facility monthly or more often. Ten percent contacted residents once a year.

There was little variation in the frequency of committee meetings. Seven percent met less than once a quarter, 83 percent met once a quarter, and 10 percent met more than once a quarter.

Volunteers' Relationship to Nursing Facilities

Data collected from the application forms described volunteers' contact with nursing facilities at the time they applied. Twelve questions assessed applicants' ties with nursing facilities. Not surprisingly, the most frequent relationship was knowing persons in the facility where their committee of interest was located. Seventy-two percent knew residents in the care center served by the committee they hoped to join. A majority (58 percent) also indicated they knew people well who worked in the facility. Seventeen percent had previously worked at a facility. Other types of connections to facilities were substantially less frequent. For example, twenty-nine persons (4 percent) were related to employees of a facility. Others had financial interests in a care center (4 percent), and 1 percent were public employees who worked with a facility in some capacity. The importance of ties with facilities in fostering interest in participation and perception of skills as an advocate is discussed in chapter 3.

Demographic Correlates of Characteristics of Participation

Age

Age was negatively related to level of education ($r = -.23$, $p < .01$). Even though level of education of these volunteers was high, its relationship with age paralleled that among samples of the general population of older persons (Atchley, 1997) in which younger persons have more formal education. Male and female volunteers did not differ in age. I considered whether age related to the context in which volunteers worked. Older and younger volunteers worked in committees of similar sizes. Not surprisingly, however, older advocates had served longer than their younger peers ($r = .23$, $p < .01$). Older volunteers tended to live in smaller communities, although the relationship was not strong ($r = -.09$, $p < .05$).

Age was associated with few aspects of participation. Age, for example, was not linked with whether volunteers had initial or in-service training. Older volunteers reported contacting each resident assigned to them more frequently than younger persons, but the relationship was not strong ($r = .08$, $p < .05$). Leadership positions (chair and secretary) within the resident advocate committees were independent of age of volunteers. There was no relationship between age and having a close relative in a nursing facility. In summary, there were few differences in the characteristics of the context in which the work of older and younger volunteers was conducted.

Gender

Most of the characteristics of volunteer involvement were independent of gender. Women had somewhat less formal education than did men ($r = -.20$, $p < .01$). Women had been volunteers somewhat longer ($r = .08$, $p < .05$) and attended committee meetings somewhat more frequently ($r = .10$, $p < .01$), but in general, men and women spent comparable amounts of time on advocacy activities, received similar training, and served on committees of similar sizes.

Community Size

Demographic characteristics of volunteers and aspects of training and participation were largely independent of community size. When they were correlated, relationships were modest. Volunteers who worked in facilities in larger communities tended to have somewhat higher levels of education ($r = .13, p < .01$). Women and men, however, volunteered in communities of similar sizes.

Community size was largely unrelated to characteristics of participation. Total number of hours spent per month on advocacy, length of service, and frequency of contact with residents, for example, were independent of community size. Committees in larger communities tended to meet a bit more frequently ($r = .12, p < .01$). Prior training, in-service training, preferences for more training, and feelings of being hindered by inadequate training of volunteers were not related to community size.

Resident advocacy committees located in larger communities had more members ($r = .33, p < .01$). A partial correlation indicated that the relationship between committee and community size was reduced somewhat when the size of nursing facilities was controlled ($r = .21, p < .01$). Even so, committees tended to be larger in larger communities independent of the size of care facilities in which they were located. Chapter 7 examines the possible effects of community size on the work of volunteers. Chapter 3 presents volunteers' reasons for interest in participating in the ombudsman program and their skills.

Chapter 3

Pathways to Volunteering

Interests and Skills of Volunteers

INTRODUCTION

Research has demonstrated that older volunteers are resources for human services programs and that volunteering generally has positive effects for participants and for those they assist (Wheeler, Gorey, & Greenblatt, 1998). Although there is literature documenting the wide range of activities of volunteers, amount of time spent, and their motivations, there is less information about the skills they bring to their roles. Yet the skills they have or are willing to employ may greatly affect needed training that, in turn, is a factor in performance and retention.

In this chapter, data from the application forms provide a unique view of applicants' thoughts about various aspects of volunteering before they actually began, revealing what drew them to this specific volunteer setting, including reasons for their interest and how they initially were informed of the opportunity to serve. Volunteers shared perceptions of their skills, observations of how they could help, and difficulties they anticipated. In addition, they noted prior experiences as volunteers and contacts they had with the facility in which they hoped to work. Completion of the application form was their formal declaration of interest in becoming a volunteer.

First, I considered how applicants learned about opportunities to become involved in the ombudsman program. A second objective was to ascertain volunteers' reasons for their interest and skills they felt they could employ as resident advocates in nursing facilities. A final objective was to investigate demographic characteristics of volunteers that were associated with reasons for their interest in or skills they believed they would bring as resident advocates to the ombudsman program. These characteristics were age, gender, education, employment status, and prior volunteer experiences. Demographic correlates of interests and skills were used to suggest areas of needed instruction and training.

LITERATURE ABOUT REASONS FOR INTEREST IN VOLUNTEERING AND SKILLS

Some motivations for involvement in specific programs may be applicable to volunteering in general, but others may be related to aspects of a particular type of program (Coffman & Adamek, 1999; Kovacs & Black, 1999). Interests that prompt participation reflect values that not only may determine involvement in specific kinds of volunteering but also may shape behavior in a particular type of program. For example, volunteers with interests in visits and contact with older persons may select involvement in an ombudsman program, and they may more likely identify with friendly visiting as a primary practice than individuals who are drawn by a clearer concern for advocacy. Research on motivation for volunteering, however, has largely assessed responses to the general concept of participation in unpaid efforts rather than to specific types of programs.

In discussing their motivations for involvement, the majority of volunteers describe some variation of wanting to help others as their primary reason for participating (Guterbock & Fries, 1997; Fischer & Schaffer, 1993). Some researchers suggest that motivation to do good for others is really egoistic because it also benefits the helper. Others conclude that volunteering is a unidimensional concept, including both altruistic and egoistic reasons for participation (Cnaan & Goldberg-Glen, 1991).

Even so, volunteers often differentiate between a concern for helping others and any personal satisfaction derived from doing good for others (Keith, 1999). In one study, 87 percent of volunteers were motivated to help other people, and 72 percent wanted to make the community a better place to live (Guterbock & Fries, 1997). Somewhat fewer persons were motivated by the opportunity to be with people they enjoyed (56 percent), perhaps a more egoistic reason.

Situations that elicit strong helping responses are those in which there is immediate vulnerability for individuals (e.g., risk of organ failure), no other available helpers, and the potential for a direct, positive outcome (e.g., saving a life) (Fischer & Schaffer, 1993). In the context of the current research, volunteers reviewed the care received by residents in nursing facilities through regular personal visits with them, where the volunteers elicited and sometimes resolved their complaints. Certainly, circumstances of residents in some facilities may correspond to the characteristics of situations thought to prompt helping responses in volunteers. Nursing home residents, for example, are often vulnerable, sometimes with few available helpers to report and resolve their complaints, and may be in life-threatening or abusive circumstances (Monk et al., 1984).

Demographic Characteristics, Interests, and Skills

Some research has been carried out on demographic characteristics and reasons for interest in participation as a volunteer. I was interested in the influence of age, gender, formal education, employment, and amount of volunteer experience on reasons for volunteering and perceived skills.

A study of correlations between age and some of the motivations for volunteering indicated that altruistic reasons, for example, were prevalent regardless of age (Black & Kovacs, 1999). Among older volunteers, Rumsey (1997) found that newer and veteran volunteers did not differ in altruism.

Among their reasons for participation, older volunteers tended to focus on personal growth, availability of free time, and religious beliefs. Younger persons more often emphasized material rewards and career development (Caro & Bass, 1995), use of skills, and gains in knowledge through volunteering (Rumsey, 1997). There was also a relationship between age and the type of tasks volunteers performed. Younger volunteers tended to be involved in direct care, whereas older persons more often participated in clerical, office work, and fund raising (Black & Kovacs, 1999).

Types of activities preferred by volunteers may vary by gender. Women expressed preferences for education and health-related assignments, whereas men chose recreational and work-related tasks (Fischer, Mueller, & Cooper, 1991). Men more often gave altruistic reasons for volunteering, whereas women more frequently noted social reasons for their participation (Morrow-Howell & Mui, 1989).

In their review of the literature, Jirovec and Hyduk (1998) documented the lifelong connection between education and voluntarism. As noted in chapter 1, educational level is positively associated with volunteering (Caro & Bass, 1995; Wilson, 2000). But the significance of education extends beyond its role in recruitment of volunteers. Those with more education are most active and tend to give more time. Education is especially linked to competencies that are useful in formal volunteering, such as verbal and written communication skills and self-confidence.

Jirovec and Hyduk (1998) observed an association between level of education and type of volunteer activity. Older volunteers with higher levels of education participated more frequently in intergenerational programs with younger persons. Education, however, is more important to some kinds of volunteering than to others; for example, it was associated with political and AIDS–related volunteering, but it was not salient in informal community work (Omoto & Snyder, 1993). The considerable skills that may accompany formal education especially prepare volunteers for organizational volunteering. Greater education also helps people attain positions in organizations where they increase their civic skills and may be asked more often to volunteer. Because of its salience in predisposing persons to volunteer initially, and its effect on the kind of unpaid activities individuals perform (Okun & Eisenberg, 1992), I expected that formal education would differentiate among skills volunteers believed they had to offer. In a similar way, paid employment may contribute to skills that are used in a volunteer setting. I anticipated that employment would also distinguish among interests and skills of volunteers. Skills may be generated in employment that are independent of education. For some, employment may foster surrogate skills in lieu of formal education. Paid work, for example, may provide opportunities to develop skills such as running a meeting that may be useful in volunteer activities. For others, prior volunteer experiences are sources of skills that transfer from one setting to another.

Because volunteers have infrequently directly described skills they believe they bring to their work, there is less information about demographic corre- lates of skills. Indeed, in one study, adequacy of skills did not seem to be of great consequence to potential volunteers. Among persons willing and able to volun- teer, but who were not volunteers, lack of skills needed to be an effective vol- unteer was viewed as a major barrier by 8.5 percent and a minor barrier by 31 percent (Caro & Bass, 1995). Volunteers may believe they have sufficient skills or that they will be trained.

Little direct research has been done on the association between clearly identi- fied competencies of volunteers and the tasks they perform. One study, however, suggested a limited relationship between skills of volunteers and the activities they undertook. Caro & Bass (1995) investigated possession of professional or technical skills in relation to responsibilities of older volunteers. Having profes- sional or technical skills was associated with driving a vehicle but not related to most other activities of volunteers, including providing direct service, serving on a board or committee, working in an office, or working with one's hands.

The present research contributes to knowledge about what factors prompted interest in a specific volunteer activity that is recognized as quite difficult (Monk et al., 1984; Nelson, 1995). This research is also important because it focuses on the skills and reasons for volunteering that individuals identified prior to the time they were appointed as volunteer resident advocates rather than simply asking them to think retrospectively about their motivations or competencies.

Awareness of the Program

One researcher has found that about one-half of all volunteers became involved because of their previous organizational participation (Goss, 1999). Another study observed that the three most effective methods to recruit participants in ombuds- man programs were word of mouth, newspaper articles, and public speaking (Schi- man & Lordeman, 1989). Applicants in the present study were asked how they first became aware of the opportunity to volunteer in the ombudsman program. The chairs and members of resident advocate committees were primary sources of information for almost half of the volunteers. Administrators and staff at facilities also informed applicants and asked them to serve (20 percent). Other sources of in- formation were used by substantially fewer volunteers, all less than 10 percent. Of these, coworkers and colleagues (8 percent), articles in newspapers, newsletters, and mailings (6 percent) communicated knowledge of the program to others. Some specifically mentioned their occupations in which they interacted with com- mittee members and learned about the work of advocates.

Table 3.1

Interests and Skills of Volunteer Advocates in an Ombudsman Program

Reasons for Interest	Percentage (*N*=699)[a]
Community Service/Assistance to Others	28
Friends/Relatives in Facility	25
Occupation/Training/Experience with Aged	17
Need for Advocacy	12
Requested Participation	10
Contact with a Facility	9

Skills	Percentage (*N*=700)
Social Skills (visit/contact with residents)	20
Occupational Skills and Training	20
Listening Skills	15
Skill in Caring for the Sick and Aged	13
Organizational and Leadership Skills	12
Understanding Difficulties of Aging	8
Familiarity with Facilities	6
Advocacy Skills	6

[a] Number of respondents vary because of inapplicable responses or nonresponse.

REASONS FOR INTEREST IN BECOMING AN ADVOCATE

In an open-response question on the application form, applicants stated reasons for their interest in becoming a resident advocate in the ombudsman program. First responses were coded into six categories (table 3.1). Two raters participated in developing and refining categories. Answers that raters agreed did not fit in any of the six categories were excluded along with nonresponses.

Community Service and Assistance to Others

Applicants' most frequent motivation for volunteering was a desire to perform community service and to act on their positive feelings toward older persons whom they believed were in need of help. A little over one-quarter noted community service or a desire to help as reason for their interest in participating (table 3.1). For example, two volunteers shared their thoughts: "I would be interested to fill a need, to be of service, to be an advocate for those that need a caring and impartial liaison." "Helping to give them [residents] a place where they can maintain a sense of dignity and respect would be the reason for my volunteering for this position."

A farmer summarized his interest in volunteering in this way: "I have a desire to share my time and abilities with my community. I'm a Christian and I want to extend compassion and support to burdened people. Because I am semi-retired, I have time to be of service to others." Another noted, "Many of the residents have no one coming to see them. People think that when a person is in a nursing home they have lost some mental capabilities and they stay away." One woman saw her service on a committee as a way to repay older persons in the community: "When I heard about the program, it occurred to me that this would be a way to give to the residents more than a friendly visit or a smile. It is a way to give back a small portion for their hard work in developing our community." Such reciprocity continued to be important as a reason for sustained participation after applicants became volunteers.

Relatives and Friends as Residents: Contact with the Facility

Although general aspects of altruism may have been the basic motivation for the participation of most volunteers, some persons' reasons directly related to contact with a facility. For example, having relatives or friends residing in the particular facility in which they applied to work or in another facility drew individuals to volunteer. Some had long-standing contacts with residents: "On visits one can be aware of both good and unsatisfactory practices. One of the main reasons I'm interested is because I care about these people. I have known many of them for a long, long time." That friends and relatives lived in a nursing facility prompted almost one-quarter of applicants to become advocates.

Occupation and Experience

A current or prior occupation, training, or experience with the aged fostered an interest in volunteering for almost a fifth of the volunteers. These earlier or ongoing experiences yielded either formal or informal learning, enhanced interest in serving as advocates, and as is shown later, provided skills to use in the ombudsman program.

Need for the Advocacy

Some applicants directly commented on the need for volunteer advocates. In some instances, this view was based on prior observation in the facility. Applicants stressed that advocates were needed who were dedicated to "overseeing care," "protecting rights of the aged," "ensuring fair treatment," and "protecting rights of those with little or no family" and the "vulnerable aged." "I believe residents in long-term care facilities are in need of advocates to see that their needs are being met and their rights are respected."

Sometimes the interest in improvement was based on observing things that needed to be altered. "At present, the care center has several problems. I would like to see it get back to giving better service. I have friends there." These perceived needs for action were reasons to participate.

Request for Participation and Contact with Facilities

Still other volunteers served because they were asked to become involved by acquaintances or representatives of the program. "Being asked" as a primary reason for becoming an advocate may have been related to their having volunteered in a nursing facility before or having been a frequent visitor in the one at which they eventually worked. Ten percent of the volunteers gave as their reason for participation that they were asked to serve. "A friend told me about the opportunity and the need and asked me to serve." Another 9 percent indicated that contact with a facility motivated them to volunteer. For these persons, contact with a facility as a motivation for participation was independent of having relatives and friends who were residents. Social ties of some volunteers included employees of the facility: "I feel most of the employees view me as a friend also. Many of them are either my former students or parents of former students."

Participation in volunteer activities might also help ensure the "maintenance of a quality facility" that volunteers wanted to "keep that way." Several expressed pride in the facility in their community and wanted to participate in order to maintain and improve it. As noted elsewhere, a substantial proportion of these volunteers worked in facilities in communities with populations of less than twenty-five hundred. Often the facility was the only one serving a rural community.

Volunteers described their views of the integration of their community and nursing facility. "This care facility is an important part of our community, and I, like others, feel it is one of the best and we want to keep it that way." "We have a facility that the community is proud of. If I can be of assistance in keeping it that way, I will help all that I can." Some volunteers had an interest in the facility as an asset to their community from the beginning. "I was active in raising money to build this facility, and it was required to have a Resident Advocate Committee. And I was asked to be on the committee."

SKILLS OF VOLUNTEERS

There is more attention in the literature to the benefits of volunteering, both to the recipients of volunteers' efforts and to participants themselves, than to specific skills volunteers offer. In an open-response question on the application form, applicants described skills they believed they had that would be useful as a resident advocate. Using procedures described earlier, volunteers' responses were coded into eight categories (table 3.1). Volunteers drew on a variety of skills ranging from social skills to those obtained through an occupation or formal training.

Social Skills

Social skills were among those skills volunteers would apply most frequently (20 percent). Volunteers who identified this skill primarily emphasized the ease and success with which they could visit and make contact with residents. Representative examples of social skills volunteers thought would be useful often focused on cheerfulness and changing the outlook of residents: "I could be one more person to stop in to say hello and brighten the days a little bit. . . . I enjoy having hymn sing-alongs, help the patients to look on the bright side, and to be satisfied." "I can make them see the bright side of each day because I love life and feel each day is a gift of God." "To be pleasant, smiling, to bring a bright light to an otherwise routine day. I like to talk and hope that would please them, but can I also be a silent visitor if that's their desire." "I feel I am very good with older people and relate to them well. I have an outgoing personality—can talk to anybody—I have taken care of my 89-year-old mother and do things for her daily." One woman recounted her possession of a number of skills, including social skills: "I have friendliness, loving kindness, patience, and dependability (unless the weather is inclement. I don't like bad roads)." A retired professional summarized some of his skills: "One, an ability to relate to the elderly. Two, a speaking voice. They seem to be able to understand. Three, ability to share and enjoy their life and stories."

Reliance on social skills is among one of the primary components of perhaps the most common role orientation of volunteers in ombudsman programs. In a therapeutically supportive orientation, actions of the volunteer may center on emotional support, friendly concern, or caring (Monk et al., 1984).

Occupational Skills, Training, and Caring for Others

Other volunteers (20 percent) planned to draw on skills they used in either a present or former occupation or had obtained through training. Caring for the sick and aged was an area of competency that for some was closely associated with their present or previous occupation. Others had assisted relatives informally. Volunteers who had these skills specifically mentioned caring for those in poor health, for elders, or both.

One person, for example, noted numerous skills that she associated with her occupation of working with the aged: "As an experienced nurse, I have the ability to develop rapport with the elderly, knowledge of nursing care of geriatric persons, basic knowledge of governmental agencies that oversee nursing home care, ability to work well with groups or committees."

A pastor observed: "In both of my last two congregations, one-third of the members were over 65 which means I have a lot of contact with older members and have seen their needs as well as those of their families. As a pastor, I care for each person and their needs. As a professional person, I also know the need to be responsible and accountable to others." A woman described how her paid work contributed to her skills as a volunteer. "I could never do much volunteer work as I had to support myself, so I usually had paying jobs, and these were working with elderly all of my life." The majority of volunteers who described skills they had developed in direct service to the aged or in an aging network had acquired them in employment. Some persons emphasized their formal training and subsequent occupations as experiences that contributed to competencies they could later bring to their work as volunteers.

Organizational and Leadership Skills

As an outcome of participation in an occupation, another group of volunteers noted their organizational and leadership skills. They emphasized analytical and communication skills. A woman in her thirties described herself as having "strong communication and human relations skills and being enthusiastic and full of energy with a strong desire to make the world a better place." The skills of some were linked more with formal training: "I am investigative, analytical, care for and about people, and I have studied aging and diseases of aging. I can organize and lead." "My skills are 'the ability to observe and evaluate.'" "Experience in an office has taught me to keep records, make reports, become organized and to work with other people. I have always been willing to listen to both sides of the situation in order to make a fair judgment." "I can type reports, interview patients, articulate my concerns to the administration and if necessary transmit concerns to higher levels of the health care monitors in the state."

A social worker noted an array of skills that could be used by the program: "One, knowledge of patient rights. Two, knowledge of nursing home regulations. Three, knowledge of community resources. Four, skills in working with people and skills in advocating for others." Another applicant stressed a blend of competencies. "I have handled all aspects of a business. I have computer knowledge, bookkeeping, problem solving, dealing with staff and patients. I have the capability of handling upset or angry clients objectively and with care and concern." Writing and problem solving were tasks some believed they did well. One noted, "People tell me I bring a different perspective to things." Organizational and leadership skills may have been developed in a current or prior occupation. Volunteers' responses that were categorized as organizational and leadership skills, however, referred to specific competencies rather than the more general reference to an occupation as a source of capacities they could offer.

Listening and Advocacy

Listening skills were specifically mentioned by about 15 percent of respondents. Volunteers often noted listening along with other skills; for example: "Listening, discernment, encouragement and empathy are my skills." "I would have patience and a listening ear toward residents."

Fewer volunteers specifically mentioned advocacy skills (6 percent) as a first response. One applicant noted, "I have intensive advocacy and negotiation experience. ... I am deeply committed to this review board concept." Some of the volunteers may have anticipated that the skills they articulated would be used to foster advocacy, even though they did not mention it directly.

Understanding Difficulties of Aging and Familiarity with Facilities

Some volunteers specifically cited their understanding of the difficulties of aging as a basis for their skills (8 percent). These respondents could identify and believed they had competencies to address the problems of older persons. They had not usually obtained their knowledge of aging through direct care. Still others articulated how they personally had cared for the aged and drew skills from those experiences (13 percent). The volunteers' descriptions of skills obtained through direct personal care for the aged contrasted with those competencies obtained through formal training and occupational experiences. For example, a semiretired man who had helped his father described the skills he would bring to the program as follows: "I have great compassion and respect for older folks—and now because of my age, they are sometimes from my age group. ... Staying and helping with my dad gave me many insights."

Six percent of the volunteers noted that contact with local nursing facilities had provided them with skills that would promote their being advocates. Some of these competencies arose from considerable prior interaction with and observation of residents and facility staff. For these volunteers, knowledge of aging and of the needs of residents was obtained through contact with facilities.

BIVARIATE ANALYSES OF PERSONAL CHARACTERISTICS, INTERESTS, AND SKILLS

I was interested in the relationship between personal characteristics of volunteers and their interests and skills. The data on interests and skills were qualitative and were coded into six and eight nominal categories, respectively. Chi square tests and percentages were used to consider bivariate relationships between demographic characteristics, interests, and skills. In the bivariate analyses of interests and skills, which had multiple, nominal categories, personal characteristics were dichotomized. Age was grouped into under age 70 (42 percent) and age 70 and above (56 percent). Education was categorized into high school education or less (42 percent) and education beyond high school (59 percent). Employment status was coded as employed (28 percent) and not employed (72 percent). Prior volunteer experience was dichotomized into less than four activities (46 percent) and four or more activities (54 percent) undertaken before becoming a resident advocate.

Age, gender, education, amount of volunteer experience, and employment status were considered in relation to volunteers' qualitative descriptions of their interests and skills (tables 3.2 and 3.3). In the bivariate analyses, age, education, employment status and amount of volunteer experience were associated with reasons for interest in volunteering. Older persons, the retired, and those with less volunteer experience more often attributed their participation to being asked (table 3.2, column 5). Greater education was associated with interests fostered by occupational experiences (column 3). More volunteer experience prompted a desire to serve the community and to respond to needs for advocacy as reasons for interest (columns 1 and 4). Gender was not associated with reasons for interest in volunteering.

Age, education, employment, and volunteer experience were associated with skills volunteers believed could offer as resident advocates (table 3.3). Younger persons emphasized organizational and leadership abilities, whereas older volunteers tended to note their social skills (columns 1 and 4). Individuals with less education emphasized social skills and minimized competencies obtained from an occupation or training (columns 1 and 2). Greater volunteer experience was less often associated with skills attributed to training and more often with organizational and leadership capacities (columns 2 and 4).

MULTIVARIATE ANALYSES OF INTERESTS AND SKILLS

Discriminant analyses were used to determine how age, education, employment status, and volunteer experience simultaneously differentiated among reasons for interest and skills given by applicants. In the multivariate analyses, gender and employment status were dichotomized, whereas age, education, and volunteer experience were coded as continuous variables. Discriminant analysis is a multivariate statistical technique that may be employed to identify characteristics that differentiate among two or more groups. Standardized discriminant function coefficients indicate the relative contribution of a particular variable to the function. The interpretation of these coefficients is similar to that given to beta weights in multiple regression. Coefficients, then, represent the relative discriminating power of a variable when others are simultaneously

Table 3.2
Demographic Characteristics and Reasons for Interest of Volunteers

	Community Service (N=198) Percent	Friends/ Relatives in Facility (N=174) Percent	Occupation/ Experience with Aged (N=118) Percent	Need for Advocacy (N=82) Percent	Requested Participation (N=67) Percent	Contact with a Facility (N=60) Percent	χ^2
Age							
Younger	30	27	18	12	6	8	15.71, 5 df, p<.01
Older	28	23	15	11	14	9	
Gender							
Male	35	22	12	12	12	7	8.12, 5 df, ns
Female	27	25	19	11	10	9	
Education							
Low	30	26	13	9	10	12	12.97, 5 df, p<.05
High	28	24	19	12	10	6	
Employment							
Employed	28	31	17	11	6	7	10.45, 5 df, p<.10
Not employed	29	22	16	12	12	9	
Volunteer Experience							
Low	25	26	19	8	14	9	18.59, 5 df, p<.001
High	32	24	15	14	8	8	

Table 3.3
Demographic Characteristics and Skills of Volunteers

	Social Skills (N=137) Percent	Occupational Skills/Training (N=139) Percent	Care for Sick and Aged (N=90) Percent	Organizational/ Leadership Skills (N=85) Percent	Listening Skills (N=106) Percent	Understanding Difficulties of Aging (N=58) Percent	Familiarity with Facilities (N=42) Percent	Advocacy Skills (N=43) Percent	χ^2
Age									
Younger	17	20	11	18	16	7	4	6	19.94, 7 df, p<.01
Older	22	19	14	8	15	9	7	6	
Gender									
Male	17	23	10	16	15	8	5	6	6.36, 7 df, ns
Female	20	19	14	11	15	8	6	6	
Education									
Low	27	13	15	7	14	10	8	5	39.71, 7 df, p<.001
High	15	24	11	15	16	7	5	7	
Employment									
Employed	15	25	12	19	13	7	6	4	22.58, 7 df, p<.001
Not Employed	21	18	13	9	16	9	6	7	
Volunteer									
Low	19	26	14	7	13	7	8	6	26.56, 7 df, p<.001
High	20	16	12	16	17	9	5	6	

examined in the same model. The intent was to determine whether demographic characteristics included in the same model would differentiate among the six categories of interests and eight categories of skills. Gender, which was not associated with interests or skills, was omitted from the multivariate analyses.

Reasons for Interest

In the analysis of reasons for interest, there were two significant functions (table 3.4). Inspection of the first function showed that discriminant function coefficients for age (.67) and volunteer experience (.73) differentiated among reasons for participation (table 3.4, column 1). The reasons for interest that were most differentiated from one another by age and volunteer experience were involvement brought about by seeing a need for advocacy (.32) and participation at someone's request (−.49) (functions at the group centroids are given in parentheses). The involvement of older persons with less volunteer experience depended more on the suggestion of others. In contrast, perception of a need for advocacy as a reason for involvement was fostered by earlier volunteer experiences.

In the second function, discriminant function coefficients, .78 and .79, respectively, indicated education and employment status differentiated among reasons for participation (table 3.4, column 2). Having friends and relatives in a facility as a reason for participation (−.20) was differentiated from having participation requested by others (.22). Those who attributed their participation to friends and relatives who were residents were more often employed than persons whose involvement came from a request to serve. Level of education differentiated most among those who attributed their interest to prior contact with nursing facilities because contact with facilities stimulated interest more often among persons with less education.

Skills

In the second discriminant analysis, volunteer skills and personal characteristics (age, education, employment status, and volunteer experience) were considered, and there were two significant functions (table 3.4). In the first function, discriminant function coefficients showed that age (.46) differentiated among the skills of volunteers (table 3.4, column 3). Age distinguished among the types of skills in the following way. Age differentiated organizational and leadership skills (.68) from those based on familiarity with facilities (−.39) (functions at the group centroids are given in parentheses). Older volunteers expected to rely less on skills of organization and leadership and more on those drawn from familiarity with nursing facilities.

In the second function, discriminant function coefficients showed that education (.65) and volunteer experience (.83) differentiated among skills (table 3.4). Education distinguished between skills acquired through training (−.33)

Table 3.4
*Discriminant Analyses of Demographic Characteristics,
Volunteer Interests, and Skills*

| | Discriminant Function Coefficients | | | |
| | Interests (N = 699) | | Skills (N = 700) | |
	Function 1	Function 2	Function 1	Function 2
Age	.67	.06	.46	.28
Education	.05	.78	.40	.65
Employment	.06	.79	.21	.24
Volunteer Experience	.73	.05	.37	.83
	$\chi^2 = 54.60$ 20 df, $p<.001$	$\chi^2 = 23.25$ 12 df, $p<.05$	$\chi^2 = 103.67$ 28 df, $p<.001$	$\chi^2 = 40.12$ 18 df, $p<.001$

and social skills (.24) (functions at the group centroids are given in parentheses). Those with less education relied more on social skills. Volunteer experiences differentiated between occupational/training skills ($-.33$) and organizational and leadership skills (.19). Persons who emphasized occupational skills had fewer prior volunteer experiences whereas individuals with greater participation as volunteers more often noted their plan to use organizational and leadership skills.

DISCUSSION AND SUGGESTIONS FOR PRACTICE

This research provides further evidence of the long reach of formal education for civic involvement. Education attained decades earlier still influenced volunteers' identification of skills they believed they offered their communities. Of all demographic characteristics, education is most consistently related to volunteer activities. Education not only affects the propensity to volunteer (Chambré, 1987; Wilson, 2000), but it also influences the type of activity in which persons become involved (Kovacs & Black, 1999; Okun & Eisenberg, 1992). Educational level figures into the kinds of roles volunteers select, but within a single program it also affected what individuals believed they could contribute. The importance of earlier education for the types of volunteer interests and competencies individuals may use both before and throughout retirement is clear.

Relationships between demographic characteristics, interests, and skills provide suggestions for practice. Use of social skills was more often anticipated by both men and women with less education and by older persons. For these individuals, there may have been fewer opportunities to derive interests and skills that for some others likely ensued from earlier volunteer experiences, formal schooling, and/or employment. In lieu of volunteers' educational or employment experiences, administrators of ombudsman and other volunteer programs who expect more than friendly visiting will need to adapt training to capacities of volunteers who have not worked outside the home or who have less formal education. This assumes that organizational, leadership, and occupational skills may extend readily to advocacy and other volunteer activities that require more than social skills with a primary focus on friendly visiting. Persons with more education belong to organizations in which they have increased opportunities to develop civic skills (Wilson, 2000). Correspondingly, Jirovec and Hyduk (1998) observed the need to devote attention to the obstacles that older adults from lower socioeconomic backgrounds may confront when participating in meaningful volunteer activities. Especially tailored educational and leadership training may prepare those with less-formal academic experience for more-challenging volunteer roles.

Earlier volunteer activities seemed to shape or reinforce skills and interests. For example, the discriminant analysis showed that persons with a strong background of prior volunteer experiences developed a greater focus on advocacy as a reason for interest. A high level of prior volunteer work likely exposed volunteers to circumstances of residents and underscored the need for advocacy among the aged. This suggests that those with less experience as volunteers will benefit from a greater focus on the skills necessary for effective advocacy; in recruitment and in early training, it is important to highlight the need for advocacy rather than primarily emphasizing friendly visiting.

Characteristics of persons who emphasized advocacy as a reason for involvement contrasted with those of individuals whose first interest in volunteering occurred only when they were asked to participate. Those recruited chiefly because they were asked by others—that is, "latent" volunteers (Perry, 1983)—may have had less opportunity to foster interests on their own. They, for example, were less often in the workplace, were older, and were infrequently involved in other types of volunteering. This suggests that a minority of volunteers may be recruited from among individuals who have limited connections to the community through formal participation and that they may have special needs for training.

Employment was associated with a motivation to volunteer because friends and relatives were or had been residents in nursing facilities. Demands of employment may have constrained the time persons had to care for relatives or friends, and for some individuals, later volunteering may be a way to repay others for earlier assistance or favors. The theme of exchange and repayment characterized the motivations of some volunteers. Persons without time to volunteer earlier had observed needs of family and friends when they were residents and hoped to help others with similar conditions.

In summary, work in long-term care facilities is infrequently a preference of older volunteers (Caro & Bass, 1995). The findings suggested that in their instructional plans, programmers and trainers should take into account effects of unmodifiable demographic characteristics to prepare volunteers better for their work. Younger volunteers, for example, may be best approached by building on their existing occupational, organizational, and leadership skills. Persons with considerable experience as volunteers similarly may have leadership and organizational skills, independent of education, that may be transferred to tasks and related needs in another organization. Application forms that include information on reasons for interest and capacities of potential volunteers may be useful in identifying personal characteristics of participants that may result in more immediately usable skills and to suggest needed types of instruction.

Chapter 4

Expected and Actual Difficulties
of Volunteer Advocates

A positive feature of this research was the longitudinal data provided by the application forms volunteers filed prior to beginning their work. Studies of individual volunteers over time are rare and often focus primarily on changes in the amount of volunteer participation or in the number of activities rather than more qualitative aspects of their experiences.

Prior research has most often focused on benefits and rewards of volunteering, whereas negative aspects have been neglected (Warburton, Terry, Rosenman, & Shapiro, 2001). There are opportunity costs reflected in less time to spend on alternative activities. Barriers to volunteering have been noted, some of which may be more prominent among older persons, such as health concerns, reduced mobility, reduced income, and diminished work-family ties (Caro & Bass, 1995; Warburton et al., 2001). In their empirical models, however, researchers have focused on positive decisions to volunteer rather than on barriers. Difficulties and barriers may more often be considered in studies of factors associated with retention or withdrawal. Preferences for types of volunteer activities may give some indication of those regarded as more difficult.

Little is known about volunteer applicants' expectations for their potential activities and how they correspond to their later practices. Discrepancies between expected outcomes and later experiences may suggest needed interventions that would benefit volunteers and sustain their participation.

One way to place expected and actual difficulties into context is to compare the variety of activities volunteers in general may perform with nonvolunteers' preferences for future participation. As noted in chapter 1, the types of assignments older volunteers prefer, activities they most frequently perform, and the kinds of organizations in which most do their work have been studied (Caro & Bass, 1995).

Perry's (1983) investigation of nonvolunteers' preferences for types of activities indicated that senior centers were the first choice (45 percent), followed by hospitals (24 percent), schools (15 percent), and nursing homes (6 percent). Involvement in nursing homes was an infrequent preference of potential volunteers. Recruiting volunteers to work in long-term care settings may be especially difficult. As a respondent in the present research remarked, "People are afraid of the 'N' [nursing home] word."

The most frequent responsibilities of older volunteers were to serve persons "directly as a tutor, advisor, coach, companion, etc." (29 percent; Caro & Bass, 1995, p. 77). Advocating for issues or policies was much less often an activity of volunteers than was providing direct service (3 percent).

There is ample reason to expect activities of volunteers in an ombudsman program will be more difficult to carry out than many of those in other types of settings (see chapter 1). Most volunteer activities do not involve critical assessments of, reports of formal complaints about, and recommended changes in the professional work of other persons.

In this chapter, I consider difficulties anticipated by volunteer resident advocates in nursing facilities prior to beginning their work. Data from an application form provide an opportunity to observe expectations of volunteers about their forthcoming activities. Information from application forms completed by resident advocates is compared with later experiences assessed after they began their work as volunteers. Similarities and differences between anticipated and actual difficulties are identified.

MEASURES

Difficulties in the Volunteer Role

Application forms for volunteers are filed and retained at the state Department of Elder Affairs. The applications volunteers filed before their selection were "pre" data, and the mail questionnaire provided a second contact. Volunteers replied to open-response questions in both the application and in the mail questionnaire. On the application form, applicants wrote about what they thought would be the most difficult aspect of being a resident advocate volunteer.

In the mail questionnaire, volunteers described the most difficult thing about being a volunteer in the ombudsman program. Two coders derived categories from the responses given to questions about difficulties written on the application form and the questionnaire. Then individual responses were coded into the categories for both questions. Data from the application form and the questionnaire were matched for each respondent.

Table 4.1

Anticipated and Actual Difficulties in Volunteering of Resident Advocates

Anticipated and Actual Difficulties	Anticipated Percentage (N=694)	Actual Percentage (N=700)
None	37	0
Adjustment to conditions of residents and emotional involvement	26	0
Complaint process, advocacy	21	14
Do not know	10	0
Time constraints	5	37
Depressing aspects of the role	0	22
Communication with residents	0	16
Miscellaneous (Own health, paperwork/bureaucracy, motivation of committee members)	2	11

ANTICIPATED DIFFICULTIES

Responses about expected difficulties noted by volunteers on their application forms were coded into eight categories (table 4.1). Categories ranged from no anticipated difficulties to concerns about adjustment to conditions of residents and emotional involvement, the complaint process, and time constraints.

Perception of No Difficulties

When asked about their anticipated difficulties, the largest proportion of applicants did not expect any impediments to their efforts (37 percent, table 4.1). Indeed, many were confident that they would not experience any hindrances.

Most volunteers gave reasons for their confidence, as the following example reveals: "I can't think of anything that would be difficult—there is a time and place for everything." "I can't think of any difficulties; I am good at handling most anything in my life." "I can't think of anything that might be too difficult after having worked in a similar facility in the past." One man commented, "As a senior citizen myself, I feel I can deal with our needs." Some based their confidence on life experiences, their being of similar ages as residents, vocational training, and personality characteristics.

Response to Conditions of Residents and Emotional Involvement

More than one-quarter of the volunteers articulated potential difficulties in adjusting to physical or mental conditions of residents, their behavior, and their prospects.

Response to Conditions of Residents

One person described conditions that were difficult for her: "I am sometimes uncomfortable about people—around people who have unattractive physical features. I am not proud to say that, but you asked." "I think it would be hard to handle my emotions in dealing with the 'severely' impaired. I think it will be a growing experience for me." A poor relationship with a resident was anticipated to be problematic; for example, "I want people to like me and if I thought they didn't—did not—it may be hard to go see them a second time." Some described circumstances of isolation of residents that would be troubling: "Seeing residents cry and be neglected and forgotten" and "residents with no one to visit."

For others, residents' loss of abilities was anticipated to be especially difficult. "It's always hard for me to watch people lose abilities as they age." In the same vein, others described "seeing the failing health of once healthy people," "watching people go downhill and lose interest in living," and "seeing older people cared for but too old to recover" as most difficult. Another alluded to a feeling of helplessness: "Knowing they are very ill and hurting, and I cannot do anything to relieve the pain or hurt is the most difficult."

One noted the dilemma of "working with friends and neighbors who have lost physical/mental capacities." Such situations may be hardest when residents are closer than strangers or more than mere acquaintances.

Emotional Involvement

Closely associated with concerns about changes in the capacities of residents, volunteers worried about their involvement and eventually their reaction to loss. Some described a negative aspect of becoming emotionally involved as "becoming attached and caring too deeply and not being able to give them [residents] what they want." "Maybe I would have too much empathy; these are lonely, very precious people." One person mentioned her possible reaction to emotional involvement: "Being a sympathetic person, I might get teary-eyed if a resident cried (I cry at sad movies)."

For others, further anticipated outcomes of emotional involvement included the "death of a special person," "losing old friends and residents," "dealing with terminal friends and residents," "adjusting to coping with problems related to final stages of a person's life," and visiting "residents that are suffering and knowing the end of life is near." Although having friends or relatives in a facility may have prompted some individuals' applications to the committee, some anticipated that such a connection could cause difficulty. "Because my mother is a resident of _____ facility, I will have some trouble being there for a period of time after her death. I may not have totally come to grips with the dying process." One man anticipated witnessing conditions of residents, helplessness, and the prospect of death combined as the most difficult aspect of volunteering: "[It is hard] seeing pain and suffering and not being able to do anything about it, and being in an environment where death is so big."

Anticipated Difficulties with the Complaint Process and Advocacy

About one-fifth of applicants foresaw potential problems with the investigative and complaint process. Discussions of concerns included difficulty in reporting negative findings, determining if complaints were legitimate, locating support for resolution of complaints, observing problems that were not taken care of, realizing that it may not be possible to resolve all complaints, and informing residents when circumstances would not change in response to a complaint. Anticipated difficulties with the complaint process were reflected in several representative comments.

Difficulty in Reporting

Reporting negative events was one part of the complaint process anticipated to be problematic. "I'm always positive in my thinking. And if I can't say something good, I keep my mouth shut." One person anticipated that reporting might entail eventual confrontation: "Confrontation is a problem for me, but I'm sure I would just report what I see and you would handle it. I'm sensitive and hate to see suffering and unequal treatment." According to one applicant, the most difficult thing would be "to be aggressive or to be argumentative to improve situations." "Probably the most difficult thing for me would be to take a bold stand in order to protect a patient's rights. If it was necessary, however, I would do it." Another applicant foresaw the possible difficulty of criticism entailed in reporting: "To be properly critical of the caring of others will be hardest. However, I generally expect high standards of all caregivers." A volunteer noted one difficulty in being critical of the work of others: "Separating myself from the staff if need be to improve the care of the patients." For another, "to criticize an employee that I may know socially" would be hard.

One person, who had considerable experience with a facility that had several family members as residents, predicted that if there were a "difficulty it would be knowing the staff so well, it may be difficult to point out things I feel should be corrected." In contrast, another volunteer noted that it may be hardest "not to be an adversary of nursing homes but to work in cooperation with the facility and advocating for the concerns of the elderly." Thus, applicants observed constraints on the investigative process that may ensue from an initial adversarial view of nursing facilities or from positive prior or ongoing relationships with staff and employees.

Verification of Complaints

Some applicants believed that determining the legitimacy of complaints would be the most difficult activity, as the following comments reflect. "I would have problems at times sifting through complaints to determine if it is really reality or fantasy." "Trying to decide if a person reviewed is telling 'stories.' " "Maybe separating the truth from the false in complaints would be the hardest." "I would have a problem believing that the resident I was dealing with was not telling me the truth. When my mother was in the care center, I finally realized sometimes she was not quite truthful with me, but it took me a long time to understand this." For one applicant, a potential difficulty would be "maybe to put down a complaint when I felt the resident was unreasonable or a complainer."

Although some noted listening as a positive skill, one man described one aspect of listening as his greatest difficulty: "I suppose having to listen to someone who constantly complained about everything or listen to a litany of problems that have gone on for years and are not germane to the present situation." Another applicant explained why she would be able to determine the veracity of complaints: "I feel I have a good listening ear and I'm also familiar with the atmosphere in the facility, so I believe I would be able to sort out any complaints from the legitimate concerns. I would not hesitate to speak out if I believed any existed."

Other applicants described actions that would upset them and prompt them to report complaints. "Most difficult for me would be if a case of neglect/abuse would come up. I have very low tolerance of anyone who either neglects or abuses someone who cannot care for themselves." "If I had to witness an elderly person being mistreated, this would really lather me. In fact, it would anger me." The most difficult would be "seeing people suffering, being mistreated, or observing an uncaring, malfunctioning, or self-serving staff."

Nonresolution of Complaints and Support for Handling Complaints

For some applicants, the greatest anticipated difficulty was not in investigating and reporting but the potential that complaints thought to be legitimate were not resolved. "If wrongs are not corrected in a timely manner, I can be difficult to deal with. I can be reasoned with, but not too often for the same complaint." "If care was inadequate and I couldn't make a difference, [that] would be hard." "If I would see a need for something and nothing was done about it." "It would be difficult if staff and/or management would be unwilling to listen to concerns or unwilling to make necessary changes—or made them only when I was around."

Some applicants anticipated difficulties in identifying persons, resources, or regulations to enable them to resolve complaints. Respondents described "an inability to find solutions to residents' problems due to regulations or services available" or "not being able to find the right people to handle the concerns I have." Applicants also anticipated sources of discouragement: "I might get discouraged at a lack of action and support," "Make management aware of problems only to find they are not corrected after a reasonable period of time," and "Appearing patient, when problems (or potential problems) are not acted upon by responsible parties." Some also felt it would be hard to let go if problems were not satisfactorily resolved: "I have worked all departments of different care centers and have seen things that went wrong. The most difficult thing would be to turn my back on something that goes on."

Unresolvable Problems

The anticipation that some resident concerns might be unsolvable was troublesome for some applicants. For some, "Being aware of problems over which I have no control" would be most difficult. "Most difficult for me would be that we are all limited in life to solve all problems." Other applicants who anticipated nonresolution of some complaints believed their greatest difficulty would be telling residents about the outcome. "Having to explain to residents that all their requests cannot be met would be hardest." One woman described circumstances in which follow-up with a resident might be stressful: "Answering residents' questions as to why changes have not taken place when they have complained about a problem several times would be difficult."

Time Constraints

Time constraints were noted as a difficulty by just 5 percent of applicants. Few anticipated time conflicts as difficulties, but after listing several other volunteer activities, one noted, "Always being able to fit requests for care review into my schedule would be difficult."

In summary, the most frequent response to the query about anticipated difficulties of volunteering was "None" (37 percent). Adjustment to conditions of residents and emotional involvement with them, including loss and grief, were anticipated difficulties of more than one-quarter, followed by concerns with the complaint process and advocacy. Ten percent did not know what difficulties they might face.

GREATEST DIFFICULTIES OF VOLUNTEERS

A second objective of this chapter is to assess and then compare difficulties actually experienced by volunteers with those they anticipated. Some of the strains of being a volunteer were revealed in respondents' descriptions of the most difficult aspects of the role after they began their work. Unstructured descriptions of volunteer resident advocates' most difficult tasks formed five general themes: time constraints; depressing aspects and maintenance of a positive attitude; communication with residents; the complaint process and advocacy; and miscellaneous, including motivation of committee members (table 4.1).

Time Constraints

Availability of time and possible subsequent overload if tasks exceed the time available, as well as a lack of role clarity, are among the cornerstones of role strain theory (Keith & Wacker, 1994). Time constraints, in one form or another, loomed large and were among the greatest hardships of volunteering. Expressions of strain emanating from the allocation of time ranged from feeling that volunteering interfered with other aspects of life to feeling stressed when they could not spend enough time with those residents who "had no one."

When volunteers commented on the most difficult tasks about being an advocate, the most frequently recognized problem was lack of enough time to do a good job (37 percent; table 4.1). For a majority of volunteers, the limitations on time related to other constraints in their lives. Demands of family and employment, additional volunteer commitments, and maintenance of informal ties limited available time and contributed to the feeling that volunteering interfered with other aspects of life. The types of time constraints described by volunteers were categorized into four groups: competing activities, loneliness of residents, time and committee work, and residents' time.

Competing Activities

Various volunteer comments echoed the remark that "the time involved is a problem" (female, age 77). "Finding time to make visits to residents as often as I would like is a difficulty" (female, age 82). "Having the time—getting motivated to get to the residence and begin" (female, age not given). Another observed the time difficulty but also noted a benefit: "Just taking the time to add to an already busy day is hard, but I always have a good feeling when I visit" (female, age 64).

As noted in their application forms, many of the advocates had numerous simultaneous volunteer experiences and obligations. Sometimes multiple demands interfered with one another. A volunteer in her fifties who may have limited her involvement commented: "I really do wish I had more time to devote to this program. I am employed full time." She then listed eight specific volunteer activities in which she was involved besides her work as an advocate. "It would be much easier to give them all up, but then I would die of boredom. Thank God for volunteers. Volunteers are love in motion." This person, as well as some others, seemed to thrive on an accumulation of activities.

Time and the Loneliness of Residents

Volunteers described how pressures of time for them intersected with the loneliness of some residents who were able to communicate. "Wishing there was time to spend with lonely individuals" is hard (female, no age given). Another woman (age 63) observed that the hardest thing about being an advocate was "visiting with people and seeing how lonesome they are; some people have nobody at all!" Thus, juxtaposed to the hardship associated with those who could not communicate was the loneliness of those who could relate to others but for whom volunteers felt they did not have sufficient time to give.

Time and Committees

Volunteers identified time constraints as a factor in the effective functioning of committees. "I find it very hard to get other members to a meeting. All but one, work. I suppose this is the reason. It's hard to put forth a coordinated effort when you don't have regular committee meetings" (female, age 72). "Some volunteers have so many commitments that it's difficult to meet" (female, age 70). Most volunteers who recounted their time constraints did not relate them to the quality of committee functioning, although a few did so. In committee records, however, it was evident that absenteeism plagued some groups far more than others.

Residents' Time

Less frequently, problems with time revolved around residents who were busy or unavailable to meet with the volunteer. For some residents, particular times were better than others for interacting with volunteers. A few advocates noted this as a constraint. "Finding the time when residents are responsive to visit with them is difficult" (female, 59 years). An 80-year-old woman found the greatest difficulty as "trying to get cooperation from residents," and another volunteer elaborated on her problems: "Explaining who I am to residents, finding residents who are not in their rooms, and an angry resident who pretends to be deaf" (female, 69 years). When queried, most volunteers indicated that residents were usually interested in meeting with them. Clearly, however, availability and cooperation of residents was a problem for a minority of volunteers. A few observed residents who were afraid to discuss possible complaints. This view was not voiced by the majority.

In summary, time constraints, which were also a significant factor in uncertainty about continued participation, were most salient among the primary difficulties of volunteering that respondents noted. Responses ranged from irritation at the interference of volunteering with their other activities to feelings of guilt at not being able to spend more time with residents who could communicate and who enjoyed the visits.

Depressing Aspects

A little more than a fifth of the respondents found the tasks of a volunteer depressing and observed they had difficulty in maintaining a positive attitude (table 4.1). The depressing aspects often related to the condition of residents or decremental changes observed by volunteers. Accordingly, for some volunteers, these circumstances affected the ease with which they performed their tasks.

A male volunteer of 75 years, for example, noted, "Sometimes it becomes discouraging to see how persons deteriorate in old age—and I have to force myself to go and make visits." "My residents were in ____ [name of facility]—the last 'stop.' It was hard to see them lose their health, or to linger too long beyond a 'quality' lifestyle" (female, age 68). Comments such as "Seeing how some residents are failing from interview to interview" (male, age 63) and "the helplessness of so many residents" (female, 64 years) reflected this type of discouragement in volunteer work.

Personal contact with residents, especially friends and acquaintances with whom they had experienced happier times, became sharply more difficult. In their applications, the majority noted that they knew persons in the facility well. Such friendship had implications for their work as volunteers. For example, the most difficult thing for some was "seeing people I have known for a long time lose their quality of life" (female, age 66). Yet this difficulty did not preclude the continuation or initiation of new close social ties.

Over time, some advocates formed close relationships with residents whom they contacted regularly. Termination of these ties was especially troubling for some and was identified by them as the most difficult aspect of volunteering. "The death of one of the residents you worked with is hard" (male, age 77).

Thus, physical and mental deterioration of residents and loss probably contributed most to the "sad and depressing" visits of some volunteers. The depression experienced by some volunteers was influenced by observing the health and disability of residents rather than by other difficult aspects of their tasks as advocates.

Communication with Residents

Some volunteers identified the quality of communication with residents as the greatest difficulty (16 percent). Reported problems with communication, of course, were not unrelated to the deteriorating conditions of residents. Furthermore, cognitive impairment may undermine previous relationships more than physical decline per se. Volunteers described difficulties related to "the ones who are unable to communicate" (female, age 77). One woman (age 54) further articulated the effect of impaired communication on the work of advocates: "When I am assigned to visit someone who cannot speak and/or move on their own, it is difficult to assess the adequacy of their care."

Impaired communication not only hampered the work of volunteers but also affected them emotionally. Among the difficulties were "the residents who don't know you're there. It makes me so sad" (female, age 67). "It is difficult not being able to talk to the family when residents cannot communicate" (female, age 61). In instances of extreme impairment, some volunteers believed residents' families could assist more and wanted additional help from them. In response to a question on the questionnaire, 28 percent of the advocates expressed a preference for more support from residents' families.

The Complaint Process and Advocacy

Other hardships related to the context in which monitoring and investigating complaints occurred. These concerns ranged from the stress of listening to some complaints, realizing their potential for resolution, and establishing their legitimacy. For example, a little over 10 percent found listening to complaints that may not be resolved as a primary difficulty.

Volunteers distinguished between difficulties introduced by complaints that could be resolved but were resisted by administration and those they felt no one could resolve. The latter type of complaint, one that perhaps defies resolution, was described by a woman in her nineties, who noted as most problematic "the things they complain about that no one can do anything to change. Most just want to be home." That resolution of legitimate complaints may be thwarted was a difficulty: "Having complaints taken seriously and getting something done about them" (female, age 72) are problems. For some volunteers, two of the greatest difficulties involved verification of complaints and unresponsiveness to complaints.

Verification of Complaints

Volunteers noted the difficulty in differentiating between complaints that had a basis in fact and those that were not warranted. Some spoke directly about the dilemma inherent in determining the legitimacy of some complaints. "Finding out if the resident is a complainer or serious about their problem" is difficult (female, age 80). "Not knowing if complaints are legitimate" is the hardest (female, age 72). "Knowing if complaints are real [is a problem]. Residents have no conception of time or responsibilities of staff" (female, age 72).

The implication is that residents' expectations of staff may be sometimes unrealistic. In other instances, legitimate complaints may be misrepresented, inaccurately recalled, or left unstated.

In contrast to "overcomplainers" was the frustration of "getting the resident to complain when things are not right" (female, age 53). "Getting the residents to talk more openly about their problems, if they have problems" is hard (male, age 71). The possibility of residents' reluctance to complain because of real or imagined retribution assigns even more importance to the skills of volunteers in observing and reporting concerns that they alone may feel confident enough to report.

Unresponsiveness to Complaints

Another dilemma in the process of investigation and resolution of residents' concerns was described as a lack of responsiveness to committee complaints. For one respondent, the greatest difficulty was that "the complaints aren't corrected" (female, age 54). "I feel our committee uses the right methods of knowing the residents, observing and listening to their needs, and taking concerns to the administration. But we seldom feel any responsiveness. So are we effective?" (female, age 53). Failure to have complaints taken seriously and resolved was the basis of problems identified by some as the "hardest" and led volunteers to question their efficacy. For example, difficulties for one woman in her sixties included "wondering whether we make any difference at all and feeling like an interloper who is just tolerated by the administration, because it's the law."

Staffing

Another volunteer described a specific complaint as the hardest thing about the work of advocates: "Observing how short-staffed the facility is (not fast enough in answering residents' 'call lights,' etc.) and the frustration of not being able to alleviate the problem" (female, age 63). A volunteer in her fifties from a different facility summarized a similar difficulty: "Our questions about care often seem related to staffing inadequacies. The administrators won't listen to our staffing concerns since our area of responsibility is patient care."

Lack of staff was a recurrent theme and one which evoked a kind of resignation in some volunteers. "Not having good help at the N.H. is the greatest difficulty. I can't be down at the home all the time to see things are done right" (female, age 65). Another described the hardship of "listening to complaints about lack of staff when there is nothing you can do about the situation" (male, age 54).

At the same time, advocates also exhibited compassion for staff in the facilities. Part of the difficulty was high staff turnover, which had implications for both the residents and staff who remained. One man (74 years) described his greatest problem as "watching the turnover in staff—seeing the over-worked staff." Empathy for staff in settings where needs for additional personnel were great and rates of complaints were higher was a cause of strain for volunteers.

Visits

For a few persons, the visit with residents itself was a source of stress. A man in his seventies commented, "Calling on residents who are strangers and not knowing their physical or mental limitations" was hardest. Another found "what to talk about" to be a source of uncertainty (female, age 77). Stress about visits with residents, more than some other difficulties, may be addressed through training, provision of information about residents in preparation for interviews, and follow-up of newer volunteers.

DISCREPANCIES BETWEEN ANTICIPATED AND ACTUAL DIFFICULTIES

This section comprises comparisons of anticipated and actual difficulties of volunteer resident advocates, drawing attention to the most marked differences between expectations of applicants and their later circumstances as volunteers.

Perception of No Difficulties

Before assuming their volunteer duties, 37 percent of the sample believed there were no difficulties that would impede their work. In contrast, all experienced volunteers who replied cited some difficulties. Thus, the confidence of almost 40 percent of the applicants that there would be no obstacles or impediments was altered when they became practicing volunteers. This was the largest discrepancy observed between anticipated events and actual experience.

Time Constraints

As a group, applicants underestimated the strain caused by time constraints. Among practicing volunteers, finding time and coordinating paid work, handling additional volunteer activities, and managing family and social demands were the difficulties most often noted (37 percent). As applicants, few had anticipated (5 percent), or at least did not mention, hindrances from limited personal time or any aspects of time as constraints prior to becoming a volunteer.

For practicing volunteers, a lack of time affected the number of reviews with residents and attendance at committee meetings to discuss complaints. Both younger and older volunteers experienced strain that they attributed to the amount of time needed for their work. Younger persons had employment and family responsibilities, and older volunteers noted family obligations. Both older and younger persons had competing volunteer activities.

Depression and Difficulties in Communication

Some applicants expressed direct concern about interacting with residents who were at the end of their lives. Although they rarely expressly mentioned potentially depressing aspects of their work on the application form, a large proportion focused on difficulties and concerns arising from the physical and mental condition of residents. Applicants phrased anticipated difficulties with residents in terms of failure to establish good relationships with those whom they visited, concern about the isolation of residents who had no family, and speculation about their reaction to impairment and deterioration.

With experience, volunteers elaborated on depressing features of their efforts and the difficulty in sustaining a positive attitude toward their work. Some volunteers differentiated more specifically and directly between difficulties in communicating with residents, the depressive outcomes of physical and mental decline, and discouragement with the complaint process. They had not anticipated the magnitude of depressive outcomes they would later experience.

In summary, perceptions about the amount of difficulties, time, depression, and problems in communication were areas that showed the greatest discrepancies between expectations and actual experiences. There was less discrepancy, however, between the anticipated difficulties in managing the complaint process and volunteers' later experiences than in some other areas.

SUMMARY AND IMPLICATIONS FOR PRACTICE

Information from applications and data gathered later in a questionnaire provided a longitudinal perspective that permitted the assessment of discrepancies between anticipated difficulties and subsequent, actual difficulties experienced by volunteers. Some of the differences between problems anticipated by applicants and those they later observed as volunteers were large, indicating concerns that could be addressed through training. Insofar as possible, training that addresses potential discrepancies between expectations and experiences should be conducted early in the activities of volunteers. Observed incongruencies suggested five general areas for training, some of which are applicable to volunteer programs more generally and not limited to those for resident advocates.

1. The possible underestimation of difficulties by applicants should be clarified at the time of acceptance into a volunteer program. Almost all experienced volunteers studied noted problems they had not anticipated. Because unexpected hardships in particular may be reasons for later strain and resignation of volunteers, training should include

accurate projections of potential challenges specific to their programs and ways to address them.

2. Time constraints were a prominent difficulty recounted by experienced volunteers in contrast to applicants, who infrequently anticipated troublesome time demands. Time requirements are also reasons that volunteers resign and are barriers to volunteering in the first place (Caro & Bass, 1995). Early in their contact with the organization, prospective volunteers should be apprised of the time demands of the activities they will be expected to perform. Estimates of the number of residents or clients assigned to volunteers, the number of visits or activities, and the approximate length of time needed for any type of direct service to recipients should be provided to prospective volunteers.

3. Interaction with residents was anticipated as a difficulty by applicants, and it remained a concern when they were more experienced. Both experienced and inexperienced volunteers in any setting in which direct service is provided need training in communicating with clients. Participants' needs are not exclusively for training in instrumental practices. Instruction is needed in managing the potentially depressing aspects of volunteering, including deterioration of residents, grief, and loss. These made up a significant portion of the anticipated and actual difficulties of the men and women studied. Intervention to manage potential emotional difficulties should begin early in volunteers' relationships with an organization. For this training, it may be necessary to engage someone from outside the organization that administers the volunteer program.

4. One kind of needed instruction, managing the complaint process, pertains more specifically to advocacy than to some other types of volunteering. Training should be conducted for the complaint and investigative process in the following areas: techniques of observation and collection of information from residents, verification of complaints, procedures for reporting complaints, instruction in filing forms, available resources to resolve complaints, procedures to address unresponsiveness to complaints, and communication of outcomes of unresolvable complaints to residents.

5. Inexperienced volunteers need to be assured of competent assistance as they learn and apply advocacy skills. Mentors who are experienced, capable advocates could be assigned to novice volunteers to work with them over a sustained period of time. Through such a mentoring program, newer and experienced volunteers could work together to diminish the hindrances attributed to inadequately prepared volunteers and that eventually undermine their effectiveness and that of their peers. Sustained mentoring and instruction in investigative procedures were also recommended directly by volunteers (see chapter 11).

There have been few direct studies of the difficulties of practicing volunteers. More research has focused on the reasons volunteers resign and on barriers to their initial participation (Caro & Bass, 1995). The present analysis was based on the premise that the incongruence between anticipated difficulties and those later experienced as actual problems can provide points for intervention. The significance of the research extends to various types of voluntarism beyond that of volunteer advocates. It suggests the importance of assessing expectations of prospective volunteers and their subsequent experiences in ombudsman programs, as well as in other organizational settings. Inaccurate information about the demands of volunteer activities may attract persons with skills that do not match those needed. Such incongruence may foster strain, curtail satisfaction, reduce effectiveness, and contribute to withdrawal from programs. The relationship between difficulties anticipated by applicants and those actually experienced by practicing volunteers may identify areas of needed care and training in any setting in which volunteers contribute.

Chapter 5

Social-Psychological Outcomes of Volunteering

Effects of Demographic Characteristics, Training and Education Activities, and Participation

INTRODUCTION

This chapter describes views and circumstances of individuals in the sample after they became practicing volunteers. Whereas some information on volunteer experiences presented in earlier chapters was more qualitative and in their own words, this chapter contains descriptions of volunteers' responses to their duties as revealed through the use of more quantitative measures. I consider the facets of volunteers' work that were most salient to them, behaviors that were troublesome, stressful, and those that thwarted their doing a better job, accomplishments that produced feelings of effectiveness, and support they benefited from and needs they anticipated.

In this chapter, three sets of characteristics that described the volunteers and aspects of their work are considered in relation to seven personal assessments of outcomes of their efforts. The three sets of volunteer characteristics are demographic, aspects of participation, and training and education activities. I investigated the extent to which these characteristics affected volunteers' assessments of their experiences and activities.

For the present research, I used two types of measures of outcomes of volunteers' work. The number of complaints filed and the number of unresolved complaints, which are considered in chapters 7 and 8, respectively, make up one type of outcome measure of the efforts of volunteers. Volunteers' attitudes and perceptions of their work are a second kind of outcome and are the focus of this chapter. Volunteers made the following seven assessments of outcomes of their activities: (1) importance of functions of volunteer advocates, (2) hindrances, (3) overall effectiveness in their tasks, (4) role strain, (5) effectiveness in managing complaints, (6) support received, and (7) support needed.

MEASURES

The first group of volunteer characteristics considered in relation to social-psychological outcomes were demographic: age, gender, and education. In analyses, higher values for age and education indicated older age and more education. Male was coded "0," and female "1."

Characteristics of participation included those that described something about the context and features of the volunteers' efforts. These were number of years as a volunteer, hours per month spent on all activities as an advocate, frequency of contact with residents, the size of committee of which the volunteer was a member, role on the committee (chair [1], secretary [2], member [3]), and frequency of committee meetings. In the analyses, higher scores reflected greater involvement.

The third group of characteristics central to the functioning of these volunteers comprised activities related to training. These included completion of formal training prior to assuming tasks as a volunteer, completion of in-service training, perception that more training was needed before becoming an advocate, and hindrances attributed to incomplete training or inadequate preparation of volunteers.

To summarize, the seven outcome measures used in the analyses with demographic characteristics, aspects of participation, and training and education activities were importance assigned to possible functions of volunteers, overall effectiveness in performing tasks, role strain, hindrances to performance, effectiveness in resolution of complaints, support received, and support needed. These outcome measures of experiences provide a range of responses of volunteers to their work.

Volunteers also identified seven of their current needs for training and education. These needs for training and education included "More opportunities for group meetings with other advocates," "More written materials on advocacy in long-term care," "More written materials on understanding the needs of older people," "More opportunities to attend conferences and workshops in the area of long-term care," "More time given to teaching skills and techniques advocates need to know," "More time for individual talks with my supervisor," and "More frequent checks by my supervisor on the work I do." Volunteers checked each activity or materials that would help them in their current work as an advocate. In the analyses in this chapter, responses to the seven individual statements about needs for training and education are used rather than a summary scale.

TYPES OF ANALYSES

Analyses of the seven assessments of outcomes by volunteers were considered separately. Information about the scale items is presented first, followed by a description of Pearson correlations between the scales and demographic characteristics, training and education activities, and characteristics of participation. These bivariate relationships are considered first.

Following this, a reduced model of significant demographic characteristics, training and education, and characteristics of participation were included in regression analyses for each scale of outcome measures. Only the preferences for seven training and education activities or materials were not included in the regression analyses. Preferences for training and education materials were used as single variables in correlational analyses. Preferences were coded as "0" (activity or materials not needed) and "1" (activity or materials needed).

The regression analyses indicate which variables had concurrent, independent effects on outcomes as described by advocates. These analyses make it possible to determine the relative importance of personal characteristics, training and education opportunities, and aspects of participation for the volunteers' assessments of outcomes. A summary of the most important variables associated with the outcomes is provided in "Summary and Conclusions," which follows the sections containing the regression analyses.

IMPORTANCE

The importance that participants in ombudsman programs assign to various potential activities have been studied previously (Monk et al., 1984). In this section, the degree of the importance that volunteers attributed to ten possible functions of advocates is described (table 5.1). To note their reflection on the importance of various tasks, volunteers rated the importance of the following functions that they performed as an advocate: "Making the conditions of the residents better," "Guiding the residents through the proper channels," "Serving as a middleman between the facility and the residents," "Arguing the cause of the residents," "Serving as an impartial listener," "Explaining decisions of others to residents," "Observing staff practices in facilities," "Reforming and improve staff practices in long-term care," "Occupying a watchdog position to insure adequate conditions in facilities," and "Providing emotional support to residents" (Monk et al., 1984).

Volunteers' Assessments of Importance

Volunteers rated their functions as advocates from "Very important" (5) to "Very unimportant" (1). "Do not do" (activities) was included as a sixth category. The percentages of respondents in categories of importance that are shown in table 5.1 exclude the response of "Do not do them" (i.e., the stated activities).

Volunteers rated most of the functions as "Very important" or "Important." Because of the skewed data, the differentiation between ratings of "Very important" and "Important" is noted.

Table 5.1
Importance Assigned to Functions of Advocates by Volunteers

Function	Important (Percent)	Very Important (Percent)
Making the conditions of the residents better	25	72
Guiding the residents through the proper channels	48	32
Serving as a middleman between the facility and the residents	48	40
Arguing the cause of the residents	46	36
Serving as an impartial listener	43	50
Explaining decisions of others to residents	46	21
Observing staff practices in facilities	40	51
Reforming and improving staff practices in long-term care	43	33
Occupying a watchdog position to insure adequate conditions in facilities	44	36
Providing emotional support to residents	44	45

Only two functions were rated as "Very important" by more than one-half of the volunteers (table 5.1). Almost three-quarters of the volunteers assessed "Making the conditions of the residents better" as "Very important." This was rated as the most important of the ten functions. Substantially fewer volunteers endorsed ratings of "Very important" for subsequent functions.

The second most important function was "Observing staff practices in facilities," which 51 percent found "Very important." One-half or fewer of the volunteers assessed the remainder of the functions as "Very important." "Serving as an impartial listener" was seen as "Very important" by one-half of the volunteers. Forty to 50 percent of the volunteers rated two functions as "Very important": "Providing emotional support to residents" (45 percent) and "Serving as a middleman between the facility and the resident" (40 percent).

Two of the primary behaviors thought to characterize advocates, "Arguing the cause of the residents" and "Occupying a watchdog position to insure adequate conditions in facilities," were rated as "Very important" by only a little more than one-third of the volunteers. Perhaps this reflects the more limited endorsement of advocacy as a primary orientation by volunteers (see chapter

6). Of all of the functions, "Explaining decisions of others to residents" was least often seen as "Very important" (table 5.1).

Along with differences in the magnitude of importance assigned to various functions in the ombudsman program, there was some variation in the proportion of volunteers who did not perform the activities and consequently did not rate their importance. At least 7 to 10 percent of the volunteers did not perform three of the functions. For example, 10 percent of volunteers did not address reforming and improving staff practices in long-term care facilities as a part of their duties. Two activities associated with a primary focus on advocacy—"Occupying a watchdog position" and "Arguing the cause of the residents"—were not performed by 7 percent of the volunteers.

Thus, acting as a watchdog and arguing the cause of residents, perhaps associated with more aggressive advocacy, were less often designated as "Very important" or were among those activities not performed. Persons may not engage in these behaviors because they are stressful or because they believe they can accomplish their objectives some other way. As noted earlier (chapters 1 and 4), there is some support for the stressfulness associated with actively practicing advocacy (Litwin & Monk, 1984). About one-quarter of the volunteers studied in the present research, for example, found filing complaints a source of strain.

Correlates of Importance

Scores for the importance assigned to the ten functions individually were summed to form a scale of importance ($\bar{X}$ = 42.81; sd = 4.72; range = 22–50; alpha = .86). A higher score indicated greater importance. The scale of importance was considered in relation to demographic characteristics, training and education activities, and aspects of participation.

Of the demographic characteristics, only gender was associated with assigning greater importance to the functions noted. Women more than men attributed greater importance to the total group of activities of advocates (r = .17, p < .01).

One might expect that volunteers who had training prior to assuming their roles and in-service training would emphasize the importance of advocacy and a watchdog stance more than those without the benefit of early or ongoing instruction. However, there was no relationship between prior training or in-service and the importance assigned to these two specific activities. Indeed, the total scale of importance attributed to functions in an ombudsman program was independent of whether volunteers had training. Likewise, subjective assessments of adequacy of their own training and that of other volunteers were not associated with the importance assigned to functions of advocates. Persons who attributed greater importance to the functions as a whole had a tendency to express a preference for additional training and education activities. For example, preferences for some specific training and education activities were positively associated with importance attributed to work as an advocate. Preferences for more meetings with other advocates ($r = .11$, $p < .05$), writings on advocacy ($r = .11$, $p < .01$), and workshops on long-term care ($r = .09$, $p < .05$) were expressed by volunteers who defined aspects of their work as more important, although the relationships were modest.

Of the six characteristics of participation, only two related to amount of involvement were associated with importance. More frequent visits with residents ($r = .21$, $p < .01$) and a greater number of hours per month spent on all activities were associated with a higher level of importance accorded activities of advocates ($r = .18$, $p < .01$).

Multivariate Analysis

A multiple regression analysis showed that only gender, total hours spent per month on volunteer activities, and frequency of contact with residents were significantly associated with the importance attributed to functions of advocates when demographic characteristics, training and education activities, and aspects of participation were considered in a single model. Those with greater involvement per month ($b = .14$, $t = 2.89$, $p < .001$), more contact with residents ($b = .16$, $t = 3.34$, $p < .001$), and women ($b = 3.65$, $t = 3.65$, $p < .001$) rated their tasks as volunteers as more important. Although total time spent and frequency of contact with residents were correlated with one another ($r = .39$, $p < .001$), they also had independent effects on the importance volunteers assigned to their work. These three variables explained 8 percent of the variance in importance. None of the indicators of training and education influenced volunteers' assessments of the importance of their functions as advocates.

EFFECTIVENESS

Following the work of Monk et al. (1984), volunteers rated the extent of their effectiveness in ten activities ("Not effective at all" [1] to "Extremely effective" [5]; table 5.2). Volunteers rated effectiveness for the following activities: "Assisted in the protection of patients' rights," "Established a speedy mechanism for resolving residents' complaints," "Proposed changes in facility policies and regulations," "Increased communication among facility staff and residents," "Established better relationships between the community and long-term care facilities," "Improved the day-to-day life of long-term care residents," "Provided information for legislators and program planners for bringing about changes in long-term care," "Prevented the recurrence of service deficiencies in long-term care facilities," "Alerted facility staff and administration to patients' needs," and "Supported changes in facility policies and regulations."

Table 5.2
Assessments of Effectiveness by Volunteers

Activities	Effective (Percent)	Extremely Effective (Percent)
Assisted in the protection of patients' rights	67	6
Established a speedy mechanism for resolving residents' complaints	58	5
Proposed changes in facility policies and regulations	27	2
Increased communication among facility staff and residents	40	3
Established better relationships between the community and long-term care facilities	42	4
Improved the day-to-day life of long-term care residents	59	5
Provided information for legislators and program planners for bringing about changes in long-term care	19	1
Prevented the recurrence of service deficiencies in long-term care facilities	44	3
Alerted facility staff and administration to patients' needs	72	15
Supported changes in facility policies and regulations	53	5

Volunteers' Assessments of Effectiveness

Volunteers felt substantially more effective ("Effective" or "Extremely effective" combined) in four of the ten activities. They viewed alerting facility staff and administration to residents' needs as the area of their greatest effectiveness. Eighty-seven percent believed they were effective or very effective in this function. Assisting in the protection of patients' rights (73 percent), improving the day-to-day lives of residents (64 percent), establishing a speedy mechanism for resolving residents' complaints (63 percent), and supporting changes in facility policies and regulations (58 percent) were other functions advocates believed they performed effectively.

In five of the ten functions studied, however, fewer than one-half of the volunteers believed they were effective. Volunteers in general felt less effective performing tasks that were more distant from the determination of immediate needs of residents. Less than half felt effective in preventing occurrences of deficiencies (47 percent), establishing better relationships between the facility and the community (46 percent), increasing communication among staff and residents (43 percent), proposing changes in facility policies and regulations (29 percent), and providing information to legislators and program planners for changes in long-term care (20 percent).

In summary, volunteers felt more effective in supporting changes in facility policies and regulations than they did in proposing such changes. Although the overwhelming majority felt effective in conveying residents' needs to staff and administration, substantially fewer believed they could effectively prevent a recurrence of deficiencies in service in facilities. This may suggest the need for a sustained presence or that intervention is at best temporary with limited carryover effect. Indeed, 30 percent assumed that their efforts would not prevent a recurrence of difficulties for residents. Activities beyond the immediate direct objective of improving resident care and managing complaints were handled less effectively as judged by volunteers. Some of these functions may be less part of the expectations for volunteer advocates compared with those of certified ombudsmen.

Based on a factor analysis, two separate scales of effectiveness were derived. One scale consisted of four summed items, including volunteers' ratings of their effectiveness as they assisted in the protection of residents' rights, established a speedy mechanism for resolving residents' complaints, improved the day-to-day life of long-term care residents, and alerted facility staff and administration to residents' needs ($\bar{X}$ = 14.93; sd = 3.18; range = 7–30; alpha = .76). The items that formed the first scale made up the majority of functions in which volunteers felt most effective. This scale, called Scale 1, reflects perceived effectiveness in direct assistance to residents.

The second scale of effectiveness included volunteers' assessments of their functioning as they proposed changes in facility policies and regulations, increased communication among facility staff and residents, established better relationships between the community and long-term care facilities, provided information for legislators and program planners for bringing about changes in long-term care, prevented the recurrence of service deficiencies in long-term care facilities, and supported changes in facility policies and regulations ($\bar{X}$ = 19.80; sd = 3.18; range = 5–20; alpha = .79). The concepts in Scale 2 comprised items related to effectiveness in influencing policy and communication.

Correlates of Effectiveness

Individual demographic characteristics, training and education, and aspects of volunteer participation were considered in relation to both scales of assessments of effectiveness. Inspection of correlations at the bivariate level showed that Scale 2, which assessed effectiveness in working to amend policies and communication about long-term care, was not related to any of the indicators in the three areas (i.e., demographic characteristics, training and education activities, or aspects of participation). No further analyses were performed with this scale.

Assessments of effectiveness in more direct assistance to residents (Scale 1) were independent of age, gender, and education. At the bivariate level, three of the training measures modestly related to effectiveness in direct assistance to residents. Lack of in-service training ($r = .21, p < .01$), need for additional training ($r = -.14, p < .01$), and hindrances attributed to limited volunteer training ($r = -.17, p < .01$) curtailed perceptions of effectiveness in assisting residents with their concerns.

Three characteristics of participation weakly correlated with effectiveness in providing direct assistance with resident complaints (Scale 1). Serving a longer period of time as a volunteer ($r = .13, p < .01$), holding an office on a committee of volunteers ($r = -.13, p < .01$), and volunteering more hours per month ($r = .11, p < .01$) were associated with ratings of greater effectiveness in more direct management of resident complaints.

Multivariate Analysis

Only assessments of effectiveness in more direct service to residents (Scale 1) were included in a multiple regression analysis. Although no demographic characteristics predicted effectiveness, aspects of training and participation were among the predictors of effectiveness. Lack of in-service training, need for additional training, and hindrances due to lack of volunteer training all diminished effectiveness ($b = -.09, t = -2.32, p < .05; b = -.09, t = 2.21, p < .05;$ and $b = -.11, t = 2.54, p < .01$, respectively). In the multivariate analysis, three characteristics of participation predicted effectiveness. Spending more hours per month, holding an office on the committee, and having served more years as a volunteer contributed to assessments of greater effectiveness ($b = .13, t = 3.22, p < .001; b = -.10, t = 2.48, p < .01; b = .08, t = 1.92, p < .10$, respectively). These six variables explained 9 percent of the variance in perceptions of effectiveness of volunteers.

HINDRANCES

Volunteers indicated the extent to which persons with whom they interacted or other types of circumstances created hindrances to performing their activities as advocates. They estimated how often ("Never" [1] to "Very often" [5]) resistance to their efforts or lack of support came from nine different sources of hindrances. These sources were resistance by facility administrator, resistance by facility staff, lack of legal authority, frail condition of residents, lack of support from the director or staff of the Area Agency on Aging, lack of support from the State Department of Inspection and Appeals (DIA), inadequate administration or supervision of the volunteer program, inadequate program funding, and incomplete training and preparation of volunteers.

The frail condition of residents and inadequate preparation of volunteers were the two most frequent sources of hindrances to performing tasks as advocates (table 5.3). Only 20 to 30 percent of the volunteers experienced most types of

Table 5.3
Percentage of Volunteers Who Never Experienced
Hindrances from Nine Potential Sources

Source of Hindrance	Percentage of Volunteers Who <u>Never</u> Experienced Hindrances
Facility administrator	75
Facility staff	72
Lack of legal authority	72
Frail condition of residents	23
Lack of support – Area Agency on Aging	80
Lack of support – DIA	78
Inadequate administration/supervision of volunteers	72
Inadequate program funding	66
Incomplete training and preparation of volunteers	42

hindrances, but 77 percent found the condition of the residents was a barrier to carrying out their activities. Although the majority of physical, mental, and emotional characteristics of residents may be difficult for advocates to alter, there may be strategies to improve communication that can be included in training.

Correlates of Hindrances

Scores were summed across the nine sources to obtain a scale of hindrances ($\bar{X} = 14.32$; sd = 5.33; range = 9–45; alpha = .85). A high score indicated that volunteers experienced greater hindrances in their work. Demographic characteristics were associated with hindrances. Older persons, for example, felt less hindered than younger volunteers ($r = -.27, p < .01$), and women tended to perceive fewer barriers than did men ($r = -.10, p < .05$). Individuals with more education observed more hindrances ($r = .15, p < .01$).

Prior and in-service training had no effect on hindrances. But volunteers who experienced more hindrances expressed preferences for all but one of the seven training and education activities, the exception being more opportunities to have their work reviewed by a supervisor. Volunteers who felt most hindered in their efforts welcomed all opportunities presented to them to have more contact with other advocates, obtain more instruction about their roles, and receive more written materials on advocacy and needs of older persons. Recognition of a greater number of barriers was associated with a preference for six of the seven training and education activities. Persons who indicated that they had needed more instruction before beginning their tasks of advocacy especially felt that their work was hindered by inadequate training available for volunteers ($r = .47, p < .01$).

Only two characteristics of participation were associated with hindrances, and then only modestly. Volunteers who had spent more years as an advocate reported fewer hindrances ($r = -.10, p < .05$). But those who allocated more hours per month tended to identify greater hindrances ($r = .10, p < .05$).

Multivariate Analysis

A multiple regression analysis revealed four factors that simultaneously contributed to volunteers' identification of hindrances to their work. The two most important variables in predicting hindrances were feeling that early training was inadequate ($b = .29, t = 7.72, p < .001$) and age ($b = -.25, t = -6.44, p < .001$). Younger persons felt significantly more hindered, but subjective views of the adequacy of training were independent of age. Consequently, effects of perceptions of training and age on hindrances were quite independent of one another.

Volunteers who spent more hours per month at their tasks experienced more hindrances ($b = .14, t = 3.66, p < .001$). More education also contributed to an assessment of greater hindrances ($b = .14, t = 3.50, p < .001$). Younger persons had more formal education, and they also experienced greater hindrances, but age and education had clear independent effects on perceived hindrances. The four variables explained 18 percent of the variance in hindrances.

MANAGEMENT OF COMPLAINTS

Volunteers indicated the extent to which they felt they had handled complaints effectively in eight areas. The types of complaints were food and nutrition, administration, environmental safety, facility sanitation, resident relations, personal care, health care, and protection of property. Ratings ranged from "Not effective at all" (1) to "Very effective" (5). Responses to the eight types of complaints were summed to form a scale of effectiveness in managing complaints ($\bar{X} = 30.35$; sd = 4.92; range = 8–40; alpha = .91). A high score indicated greater effectiveness in handling complaints.

As indicated in table 5.4, volunteers rated themselves as most effective ("Effective" and "Very effective" combined) in handling complaints about personal care (78 percent) and facility sanitation (77 percent). Volunteers managed food and nutrition (73 percent), environmental safety, and health care (both 72 per-

Table 5.4

Percentage of Volunteers Who Believed They Managed Complaints Effectively or Very Effectively

Complaint	Effectively (Percent)	Very Effectively (Percent)
Food and Nutrition	58	15
Administration	49	17
Environmental Safety	56	16
Facility Sanitation	57	20
Resident Relations	53	13
Personal Care	62	16
Health Care	56	16
Protection of Property	45	12

cent) almost as well. Two-thirds believed complaints about administration and relationships between residents were dealt with effectively. Volunteers felt least effective in protection of residents' property (57 percent). In each area of care noted, 4 to 5 percent of the volunteers indicated that they did not ever deal with complaints about those activities.

Correlates of Managing Complaints

In the analyses that follow, the scale summarizing effectiveness across the types of complaints is used unless separate complaints are noted. Relationships between demographic characteristics, training, dimensions of participation, and ratings of effectiveness in handling complaints were modest.

Older persons tended to feel that they managed complaints somewhat more effectively than did younger persons ($r = .11, p < .01$). Volunteers with more education rated their handling of complaints less effectively ($r = -.12, p < .01$). On each single type of complaint, there was a negative relationship between level of education and effectiveness. Gender was not associated with observations about complaints.

Neither formal training prior to becoming an advocate nor in-service training affected assessments of effectiveness in handling complaints. None of the seven specific needs for training or education were associated with volunteers' perceptions of effectiveness in handling complaints. Both subjective assessments of training—having needed earlier training and being hindered by inadequate preparation of other volunteers—were associated with diminished effectiveness in managing complaints ($r = -.20, p < .01; r = -.33, p < .01$, respectively).

Characteristics of participation had little influence on the effectiveness persons felt in resolving complaints. Volunteers who assessed their work with complaints more positively tended to have served more years as an advocate ($r = .12, p < .01$). None of the other aspects of participation were related to effectiveness in managing complaints. Again, subjective assessments of the need for greater preparation of fellow volunteers influenced beliefs about the skill with which complaints were resolved.

Multivariate Analysis

A multiple regression analysis of effectiveness in managing complaints indicated that four variables—two demographic and two subjective assessments of training—affected views of how well complaints were handled. Feeling hindered by fellow volunteers' lack of training had the most important influence on success in processing complaints. Perceptions that volunteer colleagues were better trained especially contributed to positive ratings of effectiveness in managing complaints ($b = -.26, t = -5.98, p < .001$). A positive assessment of one's own prior training tended to be associated with good management of complaints, but its effect was less strong than the importance attributed to well-trained volunteer colleagues ($b = -.08, t = -1.84, p < .10$).

More formal education had a small negative effect on assessments of effectiveness in filing complaints ($b = -.07, t = -1.86, p < .10$). Age positively influenced feelings of complaint management ($b = .07, t = 1.79, p < .10$). These four variables explained 12 percent of the variance in success in handling complaints.

ROLE STRAIN

In this section, bivariate relationships between demographic characteristics, training and education activities, characteristics of participation, and role strain are investigated. Role strain is defined as felt difficulty in performing a job or tasks. In chapter 4, volunteers described difficulties with their work in their own words. In this chapter, strain of volunteers is assessed through their responses to structured questions.

Correlates of Role Strain

Role strain was measured using twenty-five statements about possible difficulties in the work of advocates. Volunteers' responses ranged from "Strongly agree" (1) to "Strongly disagree" (5). Representative statements were "The tasks of volunteers are clearly defined," "I worry about not being able to fulfill my responsibility as a volunteer," "My work as a volunteer is very important to me," "Sometimes being a volunteer has been depressing," "Volunteers with whom I work are usually very committed to care review," "I sometimes think about leaving my work as a volunteer," "Filing complaints has been a source of some strain for me," and "Residents are usually interested in talking with a volunteer." Data were recoded so that higher scores reflected greater strain, and responses to the twenty-five statements were summed ($\bar{X}$ = 62.69, sd = 9.84; range = 31–95; alpha = .82).

Age and gender were only modestly associated with strain. Women (r = −.08; $p < .05$) and older volunteers (r = −.09; $p < .05$) reported somewhat less strain. Of the training measures, prior and in-service training were not related to strain; however, feeling hindered by inadequately prepared volunteer colleagues was associated with increased strain (r = .45, $p < .01$).

Role on the committee, frequency of contact with residents, and total monthly hours spent on volunteer tasks were not related to strain. Serving on a larger committee and having more frequent meetings were somewhat related to less role strain (r = −.11, $p < .01$; r = −.10, $p < .01$, respectively). Strain diminished somewhat with length of service (r = −.11, $p < −.01$).

Preferences for six of the seven training and education activities noted earlier were positively related to strain (see chapter 10, table 10.1 for a list of preferences). Persons who experienced greater role strain more often expressed a preference for the activities. For example, among other activities, volunteers who felt more strained wanted more time to learn skills from their supervisor (r = .14, $p < .01$), preferred more meetings with other advocates (r = .16, $p < .01$), and would have liked more writings on advocacy (r = .09, $p < .05$).

Multivariate Analysis

Demographic characteristics, training and education measures, and aspects of participation were considered in relation to role strain in a multiple regression. Only three of the variables related to strain at the bivariate level had independent effects when they were considered together in a single model.

Among the three variables, feeling hindered by inadequate training of volunteer peers was the most important contributor to strain experienced by advocates (b = .44, t = 13.00, $p < .001$). Being disadvantaged by poor training of fellow volunteers was especially stressful in carrying out the volunteer role.

The size of the advocacy committee was not related to many outcomes, but volunteers who served in larger committees reported less strain (b = −.08, t = −2.38, $p < .05$). Persons on committees with more frequent meetings also tended to note less strain ($b = -.06$, $t = -1.80$, $p < .10$). These three variables explained 22 percent of the variance in strain.

SUPPORT RECEIVED

As discussed in chapter 9, volunteers were asked to think about how much support they had received in their tasks as advocates. These ten sources of potential support are shown in table 9.1.

Volunteers noted how much help they received ("None" [1], "Some" [2], or "A great deal" [3]) from each of the ten potential sources. Volunteers received a "great deal" of support from administrators of facilities (55 percent), fellow volunteers (47 percent), and nursing staff (43 percent). Their coordinator (36 percent), their own families (35 percent) and aides in facilities (34 percent) gave a "great deal" of support to more than one-third of the volunteers. About one-fifth obtained a great deal of support from their friends, residents' families, and the state ombudsman. At the same time, about one-quarter or more of volunteers received no support from these same groups. For some volunteers, friends (30 percent), family (25 percent), families of residents (24 percent), and the state ombudsman (23 percent) were viewed as providing no assistance (see table 9.1).

A scale of support was formed by summing across the ten items ($\bar{X} = 21.79$; sd = 3.95; range = 10–30; alpha = .81). A higher score indicated receipt of more overall support.

The terms *help, assistance,* and *support* are treated interchangeably to diminish repetitiveness. The scale used in the analyses below reflected total assistance across the ten types of help.

Correlates of Support

Older volunteers believed they received more support than younger ones ($r = .15$, $p < .01$), and those with more education tended to receive less assistance ($r = -.11$, $p < .01$).

There was a tendency for volunteers who had prior or in-service training to receive more help ($r = -.16$, $p < .01$; $r = -.11$, $p < .01$, respectively). Persons who were discouraged or hindered by inadequate training, either their own or that of other volunteers, also received less support in their work ($r = -.12$, $p < .01$; $r = -.24$, $p < .01$, respectively).

The characteristics of participation tended to affect the amount of help volunteers noted they received from others, although the relationships were modest. Longer years of service as an advocate were accompanied by having received more help ($r = .22$, $p < .01$). Somewhat greater assistance accrued to those who spent more time monthly on volunteer activities ($r = .10$, $p < .05$), had more frequent committee meetings ($r = .08$, $p < .05$), and held an office on the review committee ($r = -.10$, $p < .05$). Those who were involved more as advocates tended to receive more support.

Multivariate Analysis

Five of the variables made independent contributions to explaining the amount of support volunteers received. Again, disadvantage from inadequate training of fellow volunteers was primarily reflected in outcomes of efforts of advocates, and it was the most important predictor of the amount of support received. Volunteers who were most hindered by inadequate training received less help across a number of potential sources ($b = -.21$, $t = -5.29$, $p < .001$). Another significant factor also related to training was having received formal training prior to ($b = -.10$, $t = -2.56$, $p < .01$). Those who had training received more assistance from others.

Two characteristics of participation differentiated between levels of support. Those who had served longer as volunteers ($b = .18$, $t = 4.50$, $p < .001$) and those who spent more time per month ($b = .11$, $t = 2.82$, $p < .01$) received more support than persons with shorter tenure or less involvement. Finally, older volunteers reported receiving more help than younger persons ($b = .11$, $t = 2.66$, $p < .01$). Again, age and number of years of service had independent effects on outcomes for volunteers. These variables accounted for 14 percent of the variance in support received by participants in the ombudsman program.

NEED FOR SUPPORT

Volunteers indicated how much support they preferred from each of the ten sources ("More" [3], "Same" [2], or "Less" [1]). Responses to the ten sources were summed to form a scale, with a high score indicating a preference for more assistance ($\bar{X} = 21.65$; sd = 2.44; range = 14.30; alpha = .80).

The majority wanted each source to continue to provide the same amount of support (table 5.5). The sources from which the most volunteers wanted more help were residents' families (28 percent), the Office of the State Ombudsman (24 percent), and their Resident Advocate Committee coordinator (23 percent). One-fifth wanted more assistance from nursing facility personnel, including nurses, administration, and aides.

Correlates of Needed Support

Among the demographic characteristics, only age was associated with need for help. Older volunteers noted less need for assistance than younger persons ($r = -.23$, $p < .01$).

A preference for more help was unrelated to having formal or in-service training. Only subjective assessments of training were associated with a preference for

Table 5.5
Percentage of Volunteers Who Wanted More Support

Source of Support	Preferences for Amount of Support	
	More (Percent)	Same (Percent)
Other volunteers	18	82
Coordinator of volunteers	23	76
Own family members	7	90
Friends	13	84
Residents	13	85
Residents' families	28	71
Facility personnel		
Administration	20	79
Nursing staff	21	78
Aides	20	79
Office of State Long-Term Care Ombudsman	24	72

more assistance. A need for more instruction before beginning as an advocate and feeling hindered by inadequate preparation of fellow volunteers prompted persons to want more help ($r = .27, p < .01; r = .45, p < .01$, respectively).

Only two aspects of participation were associated with perceived needs for assistance. Two types of volunteers wanted more assistance: those who had served fewer years ($r = -.18, p < .01$) and those who worked more hours per week ($r = .11, p < .01$).

Multivariate Analysis

In a multiple regression analysis, five variables had independent effects on perceived need for support. Again, hindrance from inadequate training of fellow volunteers was the most important factor in predicting need for support ($b = .38, t = 8.33, p < .001$). The most hindered wanted the most help. There was a tendency for volunteers who wanted more instruction prior to becoming an advocate to prefer more support in their current work ($b = .08, t = 1.80, p < .10$).

Age and number of years served had independent effects on needed assistance ($b = -.17, t = -4.28, p < .001; b = -.08, t = 2.05, p < .05$, respectively). Older volunteers and those with more years of service had fewer needs for help. Volunteers who worked more hours per month preferred somewhat more help ($b = .08, t = 2.08, p < .05$). These five variables explained 25 percent of the variance in need for additional support.

SUMMARY AND CONCLUSIONS

This section contains a brief summary of conclusions that can be drawn about the importance of demographic characteristics, training and education activities, and characteristics of participation for advocates' assessments of outcomes of their work. The seven outcomes volunteers assessed were importance of functions of advocates, overall effectiveness, hindrances, effectiveness in management of selected complaints, role strain, support received, and support needed. These assessments included the salience of activities to volunteers, barriers to performing the tasks, estimates of their effectiveness, sources of support, and preferences for additional assistance.

Demographic Characteristics

Of the demographic characteristics, age most consistently was associated with outcomes of advocates' activities. Usually, being older was related to more positive assessments. Older volunteers, for example, felt less hindered by the actions of others, felt they handled complaints more effectively, received more support from others, and had fewer needs for assistance.

To the extent that the assessments of seven outcomes studied in this chapter reflect how volunteers viewed their performance on a range of activities, men and women saw the results of their efforts similarly. Although these assessments of outcomes of participation were largely gender neutral, in later chapters, it is suggested how men and women and older and younger persons may approach their work as advocates differently.

Training and Education Activities

For the most part, subjective assessments of training, rather than the experience of initial or in-service training, were most salient in volunteers' perceptions of outcomes. Indeed, observations about the adequacy of their training were among the best predictors of advocates' assessments of their work. To the extent that inadequate preparation of respondents and fellow volunteers was identified as a hindrance, it diminished positive outcomes and elevated needs for assistance. Volunteers' assessments of their training and that of their peers affected almost all social-psychological outcomes that were considered.

Regression analyses showed that hindrances from inadequate volunteer training affected all of the assessments of outcomes by volunteers but one, the importance assigned to potential functions. Thus, hindrances attributed to poor training of peers had quite pervasive, negative effects on advocates' regard for the quality of their work and the ease with which they performed their tasks. Although the strength of its effects were more modest, the other subjective assessment of training, a preference for more and earlier instruction, affected most of the outcomes volunteers addressed.

Characteristics of Participation

Aspects of participation referred in part to the structure of the work of committees, such as frequency of meetings, size of committees, role on committees, and frequency of visits with residents. These characteristics of participation had no consistent effects on assessments of the work experiences of volunteers. For example, in 28 tests (i.e., seven outcomes by these four committee characteristics), there were only four significant relationships.

Among personal characteristics of participation, amount of volunteer involvement reflected in hours spent per month was most often a predictor of assessments by advocates (five of seven assessed outcomes). Some of the volunteers worked as many as forty-seven hours per month and frequently visited informally for additional periods of time. The very involved who handled more complaints likely had more opportunities to experience greater hindrances from individuals with whom they interacted. In the course of their work, they received more support but also reported greater needs for assistance. The more involved made more demands for help than the less involved, but the trade-off was that these volunteers assigned greater importance to their activities and felt more effective. The greater hindrances of those who devoted larger amounts of time to volunteer activities may have reflected that in their attempts to do more, they confronted additional barriers.

Although number of years of experience as a volunteer advocate was associated with several assessments of outcomes at the bivariate level, in the multivariate analyses, it was less important in predicting outcomes. It is important to clarify the relationship between age and years served as a volunteer and, in turn, their relationships with outcomes. Older persons, of course, may have served longer because of their age. Age and length of service were related to one another ($r = .23, p < .01$), although the variance in length of service explained by age is small. This suggests that factors other than age primarily account for how long volunteers serve as advocates.

Both age and years of service were correlated at the bivariate level, with five and six of the outcomes, respectively. Partial correlations between outcomes and each of the two variables (age and length of service) controlling for the other showed that all of the relationships remained significant. In the regression analyses in which other variables were included, however, age was most often associated with outcomes. Both age and length of service had independent effects on support received and amount of assistance needed. Younger and less-experienced volunteers both received less support and preferred more help than their older and more-experienced counterparts.

IMPLICATIONS FOR PRACTICE

1. Assessments of the adequacy of early training and education activities and hindrances in their work attributed to their own or others' lack of training together were the most consistent predictors of how well volunteers rated their efforts in serving residents and in estimating their own needs. Perceptions that inadequately trained volunteers were hindrances seemed especially damaging to the work of others. Inadequate preparation of some volunteers may place the efforts of remaining participants at risk. Persons who felt thwarted by lack of training also reported greater needs for assistance.

2. Supervisors may want to direct more assistance toward younger, less-experienced, and more-involved volunteers. The younger, the more-involved, and the less-experienced volunteers, regardless of age, expressed a need for more help from others with their work as advocates. The volunteers indicated from which groups they wanted more help. A next step is to learn specific kinds of needed assistance; some of these are documented in chapter 11.

3. In thinking about how assessments of outcomes may be altered for the better, one could focus on aspects of participation that might be changed. Characteristics of participation such as committee size, frequency of meetings as a group, frequency of contact with residents, and even level of individual involvement are factors that could be altered. Except that rates of higher involvement affected perceptions of many outcomes, committee characteristics were largely benign in their influence on volunteers' assessments. At least for these volunteers, restructuring the majority of aspects of participation would not seem to result in improved assessments of outcomes.

The assessments reported and examined in relation to committee characteristics in this chapter were subjective views of volunteers. Chapters 7 and 8 consider relationships between selected demographic, training and education, and participation characteristics and more objective measures of the complaint process reflected in number of complaints filed and number of complaints not resolved.

Chapter 6

Correlates of Primary Orientations of Volunteers

This chapter goes beyond the assessment of demographic characteristics of older volunteers to consider the significance of having identifiable versus less-differentiated orientations to volunteer work. One objective is to investigate the extent to which volunteer advocates in nursing facilities were able to identify with a primary orientation toward their work. A further objective is to determine whether selected demographic and social-psychological factors will differentiate among the orientations. That is, is it possible to develop profiles of the types of orientations of volunteers in the ombudsman program? Did characteristics of volunteers differ by the major strategies they used to address their tasks? Specifically, I was interested in how demographic characteristics, feelings of equity/inequity, perceived hindrances, and in-service training might differentiate among the types of roles volunteers implemented. The analyses provided an opportunity to determine whether personal characteristics, social-psychological attributes, or input by the organization in the form of in-service training were differentially linked with orientations of volunteers.

ORIENTATIONS OF OMBUDSMEN

As noted in chapter 1, Monk et al. (1984) identified three orientations to tasks by ombudsmen: impartial mediator, advocate, and therapeutic supporter. They observed that persons employing each of the patterns of orientation attempt to reach their objective of enhancing the quality of residents' lives, al-

A portion of chapter 6 is reprinted from *Journal of Aging Studies*, Vol. 14, P. Keith, "Correlates of Primary Orientations of Volunteer Advocates in Nursing Facilities," pages 373–384, copyright (2000), with permission from Elsevier Science.

though with varied strategies. Furthermore, the orientations are not mutually exclusive and may partially overlap. Even so, the literature seems to suggest that volunteers will adopt a primary strategy in fulfilling their objectives, but it is not always clear how persons will be distributed among the types of orientations. It has been suggested regarding the friendly visitor role that "most ombudsmen ... would hardly view this as their primary role" (Harris-Wehling et al., 1995, p. 65). There are differences in views of representatives of groups (e.g., state commissioners and directors of aging, nursing home associations, citizens' advocacy organizations, and facility administrators) about the primary duties of ombudsmen (Monk et al., 1984). For example, not-for-profit and proprietary nursing home associations emphasized the provision of emotional support by ombudsmen, whereas the opposite role of contest-oriented ombudsmen was preferred by citizens' advocacy organizations, commissioners on aging, and legal services developers. Staff of facilities seemed to have a lack of clarity about the different types of efforts of volunteers, although they tended to reject the role of the advocate (Monk & Kaye, 1982b).

INEQUITY AND OMBUDSMEN

As noted in chapters 1 and 3, a significant amount of literature focuses on the rewards and benefits volunteers receive from their efforts (Caro & Bass, 1995; Fischer & Schaffer, 1993; Van Willigen, 2000; Warburton et al., 2001). Indeed, the anticipation of particular rewards may be a primary motivator for recruitment and continued participation. Reports indicate that most volunteers find satisfaction in their tasks (Caro & Bass, 1995). If they do not have a satisfactory experience, they are likely to withdraw. In this chapter, I consider circumstances in which some volunteers' expectations for rewards were not met, but yet they persisted in the role. Specifically, I focus on the association between perceptions of inequity and the types of orientations volunteers had toward their tasks. Persons who feel they are underbenefited, and perhaps received fewer rewards than they deserve for the effort they put forth, may tend to perceive inequity in their work as volunteers.

It is important to study feelings of inequity because of their implications for psychological and physical well-being. Greenstein (1996) suggested that in studies of the household, researchers should shift from analyses of objective inequalities to focus on perceived inequity. Literature testing equity theory has established that inequity fosters distress, especially when individuals feel underbenefited (Sprecher, 1992). Inequity affects satisfaction among persons in intimate relationships (Van Yperen & Buunk, 1990), and it decreases feelings of social support (Van Willigen & Drentea, 1997).

One might expect that feelings of inequity in more formal relationships may also be associated with perceptions of diminished support. In the present research, the absence of in-service training reflected less support for volunteers as they performed difficult tasks.

In this chapter, I investigated whether either volunteers' feelings of inequity with regard to their contributions to the ombudsman program or the availability of in-service training as a demonstration of support for volunteers by the organization were associated with their role orientation. Beyond the absence of direct support through training, there is the possibility that persons with whom they interact may actively hinder the work of volunteers.

HINDRANCES OF VOLUNTEERS

There is not much literature that directly links primary orientations of volunteers in ombudsman programs with the kinds of difficulties volunteers may confront. It has been suggested that the adversarial approach of advocacy organizations and those affiliated with the national mandate for ombudsmen may curtail their ability to "serve as an ongoing constructive force" in nursing facilities (Barney, 1987, p. 367).

Growing from the possible adversarial characteristics of advocacy, the potential for animosity and mistrust of ombudsmen may be greater than for other types of volunteers (Nathanson & Eggleton, 1993). Therefore, volunteers in an ombudsman program may be more poorly received than other volunteers who may be seen as more helpful and less threatening. Advocacy has been given the lowest priority and a therapeutic role the highest among the activities for ombudsmen by some professionals (Monk et al., 1984). This suggests that volunteers with advocacy as a primary orientation may encounter the most hindrances and perhaps friendly visitors the fewest. In one study, administrators emphasized volunteer tasks as linking the larger community with the facility, whereas ombudsmen focused more on enhancing the quality of relationships in the organization (Nathanson & Eggleton, 1993). Monk et al. (1984) observed that long-term care providers were among the least likely to acknowledge that any of the functions of ombudsmen were accurate roles for them. These views may reflect resistance toward legitimization of the functions and boundaries of tasks of ombudsmen (Monk et al., 1984). Such resistance may translate into hindrances for volunteers in ombudsman programs. An atmosphere in which volunteers and nursing facility administrators tend to view the roles in ombudsman programs differently also may be conducive to perceptions of hindrance by volunteers.

That relationships between professionals working within a nursing facility and ombudsmen may potentially be constrained was noted earlier (Litwin & Monk, 1987). Social workers, for example, may be apprehensive about the efforts of ombudsmen, ranging from perceptions of duplication of tasks to direct challenges to their practice resulting in potential disruption (Litwin & Monk, 1987). It is in this context that hindrances of volunteers were studied in relation to their primary role orientation. The limited literature suggested that advocates might encounter the most hindrances compared with those who practiced other approaches.

DEMOGRAPHIC CHARACTERISTICS AND ORIENTATIONS

Available literature does not suggest directly how personal background characteristics are related to types of orientations of volunteers. Caro and Bass (1995) observed that demographic characteristics may be poor predictors of activities that older persons may want to engage in as volunteers. They found weak relationships between background characteristics and preferences of volunteers for duties or causes. Aside from being active in religion, education was most frequently associated with some of the responsibilities volunteers assumed. Volunteers with greater education were more often involved in fundraising, office work, service on a committee or board, and direct-service assignments (Caro & Bass, 1995). Education also influenced reasons for interest in volunteering and skills volunteers believed they had (see chapter 3).

Although it is not clear how education may differentiate among volunteers' orientations, based on the correlations between education and skills (chapter 3), I speculated that competencies accompanying more formal education may be preparation for the expertise especially needed by those who identify as advocates. Cognitive and speaking skills, and perhaps values related to education, may especially facilitate the work of advocates. I expected that persons who identified advocacy as a primary orientation would have more formal education than volunteers with other views of their work.

Literature indicates that gendered relationships persist into later life (Ginn & Arber, 1995; Hooyman & Kiyak, 2002; Morgan & Kunkel, 2001), although the next generation of volunteers likely will have different gender role expectations. Women's roles traditionally have focused on interpersonal care and support more than those of men. Furthermore, they may regard informal relationships with others differently. With gendered management of emotional spheres, stereotypical qualities of patience, understanding, and selflessness have been attributed to women (Belsky, 1992). "Our basic predispositions, values, expectation, and ways of reacting to the world seem just as firmly determined by our gender in older age as they are in our younger years (Belsky, 1992, p. 169). The volunteer role of therapeutic supporter may lend itself more closely to an extension of some of the life experiences of women. Consequently, women more than men may tend to implement and practice skills associated with activities of a friendly visitor.

HYPOTHESES

Based on suggestions in the literature, I formulated several hypotheses.

1. The majority of these volunteers are able to identify a primary orientation to their work.
2. Volunteers who identify advocacy as a primary orientation have more formal education and more often participate in in-service training than volunteers whose primary role is therapeutic supporter.

3. Women more than men will assume the primary orientation of therapeutic supporter.

4. Volunteers who identify advocacy as a primary orientation perceive greater inequity than volunteers with other orientations.

5. Volunteers who identify advocacy as a primary orientation experience greater hindrances in their work than volunteers with other orientations.

PROCEDURES

Measures

Volunteers' Orientations

Respondents were asked to rank order, from one to three, three general types of orientations: advocate, mediator, and therapeutic supporter. The particular orientations used were based on an earlier extensive scale construction that identified the three types (Monk et al., 1984). Volunteers were told: "Although you may act in all three capacities, think about the one you most frequently perform as a volunteer and the one you least frequently perform. Then rank them 1, 2, and 3 with 1 being the one you do most frequently and 3 the least frequently." A brief definition of each orientation was included beside the term.

The orientation respondents ranked first was designated their primary orientation. Individuals who did not distinguish a primary orientation by ranking the three types as "1," "2" or "3" made up a fourth, undifferentiated group. This included responses with ties, such as "2," "2" "2," which I interpreted to mean the volunteer did not differentiate among the activities in order of the frequency with which they practiced them in their work.

In-Service Training

The experience of in-service training was measured by the following question: "Have you received additional formal training for your tasks beyond your initial orientation training?" (63 percent, yes). "Yes" was coded, "0", and "no" was coded "1".

Inequity

Three items measured inequity: "As a volunteer, I sometimes feel I give more than I receive," "One of the disappointing things about being a volunteer is not being appreciated by the residents," and "In an effort to help residents, sometimes the needs of volunteers are overlooked" ("Strongly agree" [1] to "Strongly disagree" [5]). The items were used separately, and a higher score indicated greater equity.

Hindrances

Suggested by the work of Monk et al. (1984), a nine-item scale of hindrances was developed. Representative items for which volunteers indicated how often they were hindered included resistance by facility administrator, resistance by other staff in the facility, lack of support from the Area Agency on Aging director or staff, and incomplete training and preparation of volunteers for their tasks ("Never" [1] to "Very often" [5]). Items were summed so that a high score indicated more hindrances (alpha = .79).

Analyses

Data were analyzed using percentages, chi square, Pearson correlations, one-way analyses of variance, and discriminant analysis. Hypotheses were tested using percentages, one-way analyses of variance, and discriminant analysis. Four categories of role orientations of volunteers (advocate, n = 169; mediator, n = 101; therapeutic supporter, n = 427; and undifferentiated, n = 73) were used in the one-way analyses of variance and the discriminant analysis.

RESULTS

Table 6.1 shows that there was no multicollinearity among the variables, although the measures of inequity were significantly related to one another. Volunteers who felt they gave more than they received felt disappointment that their efforts were unappreciated and that needs of volunteers were sometimes overlooked (table 6.1). Those who expressed greater disappointment that their efforts went unappreciated also more frequently believed volunteer needs were overlooked. Inequity was correlated with only one demographic characteristic. Volunteers with more education less often felt their needs were overlooked. Hindrances were greater among those who felt inequitably treated. Male, younger, and better-educated volunteers found more hindrances in their work. In-service training was associated only with educational level. Persons with more education tended to receive more in-service training, although the correlation was small (table 6.1).

The hypothesis that the majority of volunteers would be able to identify a primary orientation to their work was supported. Only 10 percent did not have a primary orientation. This undifferentiated or mixed type was included with the other three in the analyses in this chapter. The most frequently selected primary orientation was therapeutic supporter (55 percent), followed by advocate (22 percent) and mediator (13 percent).

One-way analyses of variance were used to compare bivariate relationships between age, education, feelings of inequity, hindrances, and the typology of orientations volunteer. Chi square tests were used to investigate the bivariate

Table 6.1

Pearson Correlations of Demographic Characteristics, In-Service Training, Inequity, and Hindrances

	1	2	3	4	5	6	7	8
1. Age	1.00							
2. Education	-.22**	1.00						
3. Gender	.05	-.20**	1.00					
4. In-Service Training	.04	-.13**	-.02	1.00				
5. Give More Than Receive	.00	-.02	.05	-.06	1.00			
6. Not Appreciated	-.07	.04	.05	-.02	.25**	1.00		
7. Volunteer Needs Overlooked	-.04	.08*	.02	.04	.24**	.28**	1.00	
8. Hindrances	-.27**	.15**	-.10*	-.04	-.18**	-.13**	-.22**	1.00

*$p < .05$
**$p < .01$

relationships between gender, in-service training, and the typology. Level of formal education, gender, age, and in-service training were significantly related to types of orientations (table 6.2). Advocates were younger, and supporting the hypotheses, they had more formal education and more often had in-service training than all other groups. As hypothesized, women more often than men were therapeutic supporters.

A one-way analysis of variance revealed that the three indicators of inequity and hindrances were significantly related to the typology (table 6.2). Contrary to the hypothesis, advocates did not experience the greatest feelings of inequity; rather, volunteers with no clear orientation felt greater inequity but also identified the fewest hindrances. As hypothesized, advocates identified substantially more hindrances than all other groups.

To determine the most important factors that differentiated among the types when all were considered simultaneously, age, gender, formal education, in-service training, and three indicators of equity were included in a discriminant analysis. There were two significant functions (table 6.3).

The first significant function indicated that advocates were differentiated from the other three types especially by their age and formal education. These variables distinguished among the types when all other variables were considered. Advocates were significantly younger than persons in the other three groups, even though their average age was 67 years. In contrast, volunteers with undifferentiated orientations were the oldest of all groups ($\bar{X}$ = 74 years of age).

Advocates had higher levels of education than persons in any other orientation, whereas volunteers who were uncertain about their orientation toward their tasks had the least amount of formal schooling. In-service training differentiated among the orientations in the first function but to a lesser extent than age and education. Those with ambiguous views of their primary tasks least often had in-service training (53 percent), followed by mediators (56 percent). Sixty-three percent of the therapeutic supporters had additional training, and advocates most often had further training during their volunteer experience (73 percent).

Inspection of the second significant function revealed that gender and two indicators of equity distinguished among the patterns. In the second function, therapeutic supporters were differentiated from the other groups. Volunteers with this orientation were more often women, and they experienced feelings of greater equity. They felt more appreciated and did not believe they put forth a disproportionate amount of effort for their rewards. In the multivariate analysis, feeling that the needs of volunteers were overlooked did not differentiate among the types (table 6.2).

The next step was to determine how hindrances might be related to the profiles of volunteers' orientations when all other variables were considered. In a second discriminant analysis, a measure of hindrances was included along with demographic characteristics, in-service training, and indicators of inequity (data are not shown). Again, there were two significant functions (X^2 = 98.85,

Table 6.2

Volunteers' Orientations by Demographic Characteristics, In-Service Training, Inequity, and Hindrances (One-Way Analyses of Variance and Chi Squares)

Volunteers Orientations

	Undifferentiated	Advocate	Mediator	Therapeutic Supporter	F	χ^2
Age ($\bar{x}$, Years)	74.10	67.01	71.44	70.18	8.66***	
Education ($\bar{x}$)	2.82	3.73	3.10	3.31	7.20***	
Gender (%):						
Male	11.7	23.4	18.6	46.3		10.07*
Female	10.0	21.1	11.2	57.7		
In-Service Training (% yes)	53.1	73.3	56.4	62.6		12.88**
Inequity ($\bar{x}$):						
Give more than receive	3.23	3.43	3.52	3.62	4.50**	
Not appreciated	3.65	3.92	3.80	3.99	4.25**	
Volunteer needs overlooked	3.00	3.36	3.07	3.31	4.25**	
Hindrances ($\bar{x}$)	12.48	16.07	14.18	14.02	8.33***	

*$p < .05$
**$p < .01$
***$p < .001$

Table 6.3

Discriminant Analysis of Volunteers' Orientations and Demographic Characteristics, In-Service Training, and Inequity

Discriminant Function Coefficients

	(First Function)	(Second Function)
Age	-.59	--
Education	.40	--
Gender	--	.54
In-Service Training	-.39	--
Inequity:		
Give more than receive	--	.46
Not appreciated	--	.43
Volunteer needs overlooked	--	--
	$\chi^2 = 83.05$, 21 df, $p<.001$	$\chi^2 = 21.74$, 12 df, $p<.05$

24 df, p < .001; X^2 = 27.86; 14 df, p < .05). In this analysis, when all variables were considered, hindrances, included in the first function, were most important in differentiating among the types. Except that hindrances were most important in the first function, patterns of variables in the two functions found in the first analysis remained unchanged. The hypothesis that greater hindrances would differentiate advocates from others was supported.

DISCUSSION

This research indicates that the majority of volunteers can identify a primary orientation in their practices. In contrast to the suggestion that most would abjure the tasks of a friendly visitor and opt for a clearer advocacy role, the majority tended to act most frequently as therapeutic supporters (Harris-Wehling et al., 1995).

This chapter provides evidence that role orientations of volunteers had demonstrable profiles. Multivariate analyses indicated that profiles of two volunteer orientations were most clearly differentiated from other types. Advocates were distinguished from all others by their youth, formal education, in-service training, and greater hindrances. Their education and in-service training may have provided the background skills, motivation, and specific training to carry out the tasks of advocacy. There is some support for literature that suggests that advocacy may engender more conflict than other strategies (Barney, 1987; Nathanson & Eggleton, 1993), with the result that volunteers may feel thwarted by the actions of others. But they persisted despite interference.

The life worlds of volunteering for persons with orientations as advocates and therapeutic supporters seem quite contrasting. They were differentiated by resources they brought to the task, how their skills were developed once they became volunteers, and their eventual strategies. Finally, identification of the different primary orientations reflects divergent underlying ideologies about approaches to the work in an ombudsman program.

From these available data, it was not clear whether orientations toward ombudsmen's tasks were present prior to becoming a volunteer or whether they were fostered through interaction with others and through in-service training. Even if in-service training did not generate views of advocacy, it may have provided skills to act on the existing ideology. Ongoing training differentiated the contributions of advocates from the other types. Certainly, in-service training may be most amenable to intervention by practitioners.

Women's roles are defined by nurturing and caring for others (Herzog & Markus, 1999). Relationships with others are more salient in women's identities than they are in those of men. Thoughts, feelings, and needs of others shape the moral decisions and social interaction of women more than for men (Herzog & Markus, 1999).

Perhaps extending traditional conceptions of gender roles through the life course (Belsky, 1992; Morgan & Kunkel, 2001), women more often practiced skills as therapeutic supporters. This orientation may most closely employ caring roles often attributed to women—provision of empathy, support, or companionship. Although no direct measures of gender role attitudes or activities for these volunteers were available, skills of a friendly visitor or therapeutic supporter may be continuations of already dominant activities of women with this orientation. Congruency between gender roles and volunteer tasks may explain in part why female volunteers who primarily provided emotional support and emphasized friendly visiting in their relationships with residents felt less inequity in their work in the ombudsman program. Feelings of equity and reward were more often the purview of therapeutic supporters, and their efforts less frequently met with great hindrances.

The multivariate analysis revealed that those volunteers who did not identify a primary orientation differed most from the advocates because they were older, had less formal education, and had less in-service training. They also experienced fewest hindrances. Persons with no primary orientation may have collaborated with other volunteers with more solidified orientations who would take responsibility for resolving complaints, enabling the former to be the least hindered. At the same time, volunteers with no primary orientation tended to experience feelings of inequity. They felt that their needs were overlooked and that they were not appreciated. This group may especially benefit from in-service training emphasizing techniques that volunteers need. To the extent that inequity reflects or fosters distress, volunteers without a primary orientation to their work may have derived the least satisfaction from their efforts. The findings suggest that if an objective is to have more volunteers pursue advocacy as a primary orientation, in-service training especially will need to be addressed to somewhat older, less-educated volunteers. A portion of the training might deal with expected hindrances and ways to manage them.

Women were no less likely to be advocates than were men, but for some their major skills as a friendly visitor may be difficult to shift to advocacy. Furthermore, the gratification from being a therapeutic supporter or friendly visitor may parallel most closely the reasons some persons volunteer in the first place—to garner positive feelings from being with and bringing cheer and help to others. The intrinsic rewards from friendly visiting may be more immediate than those from advocacy. Perceived imbalances between investments persons make and outcomes of their relationships with those whom they help contribute to burnout (Schaufeli & Janczur, 1994). Volunteers' orientations may foster burnout (Litwin & Monk, 1984). Subjective feelings of inequity are important because of their potential connection with exhaustion, burnout, and turnover. Future research on volunteers can establish whether organizational support, subjective stress in the work setting, and burnout operate the same way as they do among paid employees (Maslach, Schaufeli, & Leiter, 2001; Parker & Kulik, 1995).

The importance of volunteering for elders' own well-being and their contributions to the society at large is now well established (Van Willigen, 2000; Wilson, 2000). The future of volunteering will likely shape the quality of later life not only of those who participate but also of those whom they serve. This research suggests the significance of volunteers' orientations for their efforts beyond the specific context of volunteering studied. As in paid employment, orientations of those who do volunteer work have implications for their well-being and their practices. It is time to explore more fully what older persons may expect as they try to manage challenging and fulfilling roles as volunteers.

Chapter 7

Advocacy for the Aged in the Country and in the City

Projected growth of the aged population, greater concentrations of older persons in some rural communities, increased needs for long-term health care of the aged, and continued abuse of nursing home residents are well documented (Bull, 1998; Huber et al., 2000; Krout, 1994). Volunteers observed care of the aged in rural and urban nursing homes. A primary focus of this chapter is the influence of community size on the role orientations of volunteers (advocate or friendly visitor) and on informal social ties with nursing facility employees and residents, and joint effects of these variables on reported complaints. The research addressed in part the lack of empirical data on important aspects of the long-term care system in rural areas noted by others (Coward, Netzer, & Peek, 1996). Accordingly, the investigation contributes to the comparative literature on the circumstances of older persons in rural and urban places (Bull, 1998).

Some questions guided the research: "Did rural and urban volunteers in an ombudsman program differ from one another in their orientations to their work and their informal social ties with staff and residents in nursing facilities?" "Were the outcomes of the work of volunteers on behalf of long-term care residents different in rural and urban communities?" "What factors affected the outcomes of efforts of volunteers in rural and urban communities?"

NURSING FACILITIES IN RURAL AND URBAN AREAS

There are proportionally more nursing home beds available per one thousand older persons in nonmetropolitan places than in urban areas (Coward, Duncan, & Uttaro, 1996; Shaughnessy, 1994), and there is greater usage of nursing facilities in rural areas (Peek, Coward, Lee, & Zsembik, 1997). Rural nursing facilities are smaller and traditionally have employed fewer skilled persons. Beyond their obvious provision of care, nursing facilities in rural and urban places may serve somewhat different functions. Because some types of health care services may be more limited, rural residents may enter nursing facilities when they have less functional impairment than persons in urban areas with better access to a range of services including home care options (Peek et al., 1997). The absence of some health care options in rural areas, then, may prompt greater use of nursing facilities. Nursing homes, for example, may provide the equivalent of assisted living in some communities (Rowles, 1996).

There are contrasting views of the place nursing homes occupy in rural communities. The prevalent image of rural nursing homes "is of an institution separated from its community context" (Rowles, 1996, p. 115). This motif features the nursing facility as a place to put people away from the rest of the community and as a place to die in isolation. To some extent, separation of nursing home residents from nonresidents and views of the nursing facility as an organization with few exchanges and little connectedness to the community may have traditionally characterized both rural and urban nursing homes. Recently, this view of rural nursing facilities has been challenged (Rowles, 1996). "Our society harbors the opinion that rural health care is of lower quality than the care available in large cities" (Rowles, Beaulieu, & Myers, 1996, p. 8); rural nursing homes, however, may have some advantages over those in urban places.

All long-term care facilities are not segregated from their communities. In a case study of a rural facility, investigators found considerable exchanges between residents and community members (Rowles, 1996). The nursing facility was very much integrated into the community. This connection was further manifested by numerous kinship linkages between staff, residents, and community members (Rowles, 1996). There was the expectation of high family involvement with residents. That community members viewed the facility as "our nursing home" illustrates the psychological integration of the facility in the community. Permeability of the community and the facility was exhibited in three ways: relatives and friends took residents of the facility into the community for various activities; staff also took residents outside for more formal trips, and there was a constant stream of visitors including students, family members, and representatives of other groups. Rowles (1996, pp. 118–119) described the "blending of the community with its long-term care facility. . . . The facility reveals a plethora of characteristics that might form the basis of an enlightened philosophy of long-term care consistent with rural culture and values." A high level of institutional permeability between the facility and the care facility was exemplified by the constant exchange of persons and communication. Rowles suggested that the nursing facility separated from its community is an urban-based image and may not be descriptive of many contemporary rural nursing facilities. "Rural nursing homes, because of a higher propensity for personal associations between residents and patients ... possess great potential for the development of an ethos of personalization" (121).

In rural communities, there is often only one nursing facility, and it has special meaning to some citizens. The integration of facilities into the communities and sentiments about them frequently may be reasons for volunteering in the first place.

The potentially closer relationships between community members and staff in rural nursing facilities raises the question of the possible effect of greater familiarity on decisions volunteers make. That is, will the work of volunteers in ombudsman programs be facilitated or compromised by informal social ties more in rural compared with urban areas? Is the personalization thought to be greater in rural communities antithetical to the objectivity needed by volunteers in ombudsman programs? Monk and Kaye (1982a) noted that objectivity and independence are valued strengths of volunteers in ombudsman programs. Although they did not describe the potential conflict between objectivity needed for advocacy and informal social ties of volunteers and facility staff, Schiman and Lordeman (1989) recommended against placing volunteers where friends and relatives were residents. Placement of volunteers in facilities where they have close social ties with staff may be minimized, but it may be especially difficult to do in smaller communities.

Netting and Hinds (1989, p. 421) noted that there has been little "attempt to address the advantages and difficulties encountered in implementing the [ombudsman] program in predominately rural communities." They suggested that even in urban areas—where long-term care facilities are perhaps somewhat more accessible to volunteers and recruitment, retention, and coordination may be managed in greater proximity—there are difficulties in implementing programs. In some rural areas, participation may be complicated by distance, poorer transportation, or less availability of skilled volunteers (Bull, 1998). Furthermore, an orientation toward advocacy may be more antithetical to informal relationships or a culture of "familiarity" that may be prevalent in rural areas (Bull, 1998).

Literature on the differential place of nursing facilities in rural and urban communities, advantages and disadvantages of volunteers' informal relationships with facility personnel, and the potential difficulties of implementing an orientation toward advocacy suggested a number of hypotheses.

HYPOTHESES

I. Characteristics of Volunteers

1. Volunteers whose primary role orientation is advocacy are located more often in urban areas than those with other orientations.

2. Rural volunteers have more informal ties with staff and residents of nursing facilities than do their urban counterparts.

II. Outcomes of the Work of Volunteers

   3. Volunteers in rural areas report fewer complaints than do their urban counterparts.

   4. The optimal conditions for reporting complaints are among urban volunteers
whose primary orientation is advocacy and who have fewer informal ties with
staff and residents of nursing facilities.

MEASURES

Complaints

Complaints reported by volunteers for the facility in which they worked
were coded from quarterly records over a two-year period. These records ($n =$
1,886) were obtained on-site at the eight Area Agencies on Aging in which volunteers served. To a great extent, the frequency of types of complaints paralleled those reported nationally (Harris-Wehling et al., 1995). Committees most
often reported complaints or concerns about resident care (62 percent), followed by complaints about resident rights (36 percent), building, sanitation,
and laundry (34 percent), and concerns about administrative practices (30 percent). Other types of complaints were much less frequently reported. The average number of complaints was calculated per ten beds in a facility ($\bar{X} = 1.23$, sd
$= 1.87$; range $= 0$–19.80).

Volunteers' Orientations

Volunteers who identified one of the three general types of orientations (advocate, mediator, or therapeutic supporter) were included in the analyses for
this chapter. The procedure used to determine the primary orientation of volunteers is described in chapter 6. Individuals who did not distinguish a primary
orientation by ranking the three types as "1," "2," or "3" were omitted ($n =$
73). In analyses that included primary role orientation, the sample size was 633.

Therapeutic supporters included those persons identified as friendly visitors.
Preliminary analyses showed that mediators and friendly visitors were more
similar and differed from advocates on several indices. In the analyses for this
research, two groups of role orientations were used: advocates ($n = 155$, 24 percent) and friendly visitors/mediators ($n = 478$, 76 percent). Of the latter group,
only 14 percent identified as mediators. In this chapter, persons in the second
group are referred to as friendly visitors.

Volunteers' Relationship to Nursing Facilities

Secondary data were collected from the application forms that individuals
filed at the time they applied to become volunteers. Data were coded from

records at the state's Department of Elder Affairs. Two measures assessed the informal ties of applicants with the nursing facilities in which they later worked. Information from application forms was matched with volunteers' questionnaire data. Volunteers indicated if they knew staff well who worked in the facility where they later served and if they knew residents. The most frequent relationship was knowing residents in the facility where volunteers later worked. Seventy-two percent knew residents in the care center in which they wanted to work. A majority (58 percent) also knew employees of the facility well. These two variables were coded "0" (know no one) and "1" (know residents or know employees well).

Community Size

The size of communities in which volunteers carried out their work was coded into six categories: (1) 999 or less (10 percent); (2) 1,000–2,499 (26 percent); (3) 2,500–9,999 (32 percent); (4) 10,000–49,999 (17 percent); (5) 50,000–99,999 (7 percent); and (6) 100,000–249,000 (8 percent). The average facility was located in a community with a population of 2,500 to less than 10,000. Thirty-six percent of the volunteers worked in rural communities with populations less than 2,500.

ANALYSES

Data were analyzed using percentages, chi square, t tests, and analyses of variance. Hypotheses were tested using percentages, t tests, and analyses of variance. Two categories of volunteers' orientation (advocate and friendly visitor/mediator) were used in the analyses. In analyses of variance, community size in which facilities were located was coded into two groups, 2,499 or less (rural) and 2,500 and above (urban). In a t test, population codes ranging from 1 to 6 were used. The six categories of education were coded 1–6.

RESULTS

Relationships between size of place and volunteers' role orientation, informal ties with facilities, and outcomes of their work are shown in table 7.1. Initially, the bivariate hypotheses were tested. Volunteers with a primary role orientation of advocacy tended to work slightly more often in facilities located in larger communities ($\chi^2 = 3.21$, 1 df, $p < .10$; table 7.1). In another test of the first hypothesis, a t test using the two volunteer orientations as the groups and population categories of 1–6 as the dependent variable provided only modest support ($t = 1.99$, $p < .05$). Volunteers who emphasized friendly visiting served only a little more often in rural places with populations of less than 2,500. Re-

Table 7.1

Community Size, Role Orientation, Informal Ties, and Outcomes of the Work of Volunteers

	Community Size		
	Rural[a] (n = 155)	Urban (n = 478)	Tests of Significance
Control Variables			
Age ($\bar{x}$)	69.45	69.34	$t = .14$, ns
Education ($\bar{x}$)	3.17	3.44	$t = 2.19$, $p<.05$
Profit facilities (%)	63.0	51.5	$\chi^2 = 8.74$, 1 df, $p<.001$
Nonprofit facilities (%)	37.0	48.5	
Role Orientation (%)			
Advocate	20.4	26.8	$\chi^2 = 3.21$, 1 df, $p<.10$
Friendly visitor	79.6	73.2	
Informal Ties (%)			
Know employees well	69.3	52.4	$\chi^2 = 18.98$, 1 df, $p<.001$
Know residents	81.0	66.0	$\chi^2 = 14.67$, 1df, $p<.001$
Outcomes of Volunteers' Work ($\bar{x}$)			
Complaints	1.10	1.30	$t = 1.33$, ns

[a] Rural communities had fewer than 2,500 residents.

gardless of the size of place, the majority of volunteers identified friendly visiting as their primary orientation (table 7.1).

As hypothesized, rural more often than urban volunteers knew facility staff well ($\chi^2 = 18.98$, 1 df, $p < .001$). Sixty-nine percent of rural volunteers knew employees well, compared with 52 percent of urban volunteers who were well acquainted with staff. Further supporting the second hypothesis, 81 percent of rural volunteers were acquainted with residents, compared with about two-thirds of volunteers in urban areas ($\chi^2 = 14.67$, 1 df, $p < .001$; table 7.1).

I had expected that rural volunteers would be less likely to report complaints. Serving in a facility in a rural area alone was not sufficient to impact decisions to report complaints (table 7.1).

A multiple regression and ANOVA were used to test the final hypothesis that urban volunteers who identified with advocacy and who did not know nursing facility staff and residents reported more complaints. To consider the relationship between the number of complaints and all of the other variables simultaneously,

Table 7.2

Multiple Regression of Reported Complaints and Community Size, Volunteer Role Orientation, and Informal Ties with Facility Staff and Residents

	R	β	Beta	t	p
Level 1					
Age	-.17	-.13	-.16	-4.10	.001
Education	-.06	.005	.05	1.14	ns
Profit (0)/Nonprofit facilities (1)	-.12	-.46	-.12	-3.03	.001
R^2 = .050					
Level 2					
Community Size	.17	.22	.15	3.96	.001
Volunteer Role Orientation	-.21	-.75	-.17	-4.36	.001
Informal ties with staff	-.11	-.37	-.10	-2.31	.05
Informal ties with residents	-.05	.14	.03	.82	ns
R^2 = .065					
Total R^2 = .115					

a hierarchical multiple regression was used (table 7.2). Age, education, and the profit-nonprofit status of the facility formed the first block, and their effects were controlled. Role orientations, community size, and informal ties with facility staff and residents made up the second block. Inspection of the multiple regression indicated that older volunteers made fewer complaints. Corresponding to findings about deficiencies reported by state surveyors (Harrington, Zimmerman, Karon, Robinson, & Beutel, 2000), there were fewer complaints in nonprofit facilities (table 7.2). Education of volunteers was not related to reported complaints. Community size, role orientation, and informal ties with staff had independent effects on the number of complaints. The hypothesis, however, specified interaction effects between community size, role orientation, and informal ties with staff and residents. Informal ties with residents were not associated with the number of complaints (table 7.2) and were excluded from subsequent analyses.

In an analysis of variance, a regression solution was used in which covariates (age, education, and profit-nonprofit status of facilities), factors (volunteers' role orientation, rural-urban, and volunteers' informal ties with facility employees), and interactions were considered simultaneously. Thus, a 2 (rural-urban) × 2 (advocate–friendly visitor) × 2 (know employees well, "yes," "no") interaction was tested.

A significant three-way interaction (rural-urban × role orientation × informal ties with facility staff) partially confirmed the hypothesis ($F = 8.75$, $p <$ .001) that a combination of factors created the conditions in which volunteers were the most active in reporting complaints. Conditions that were most optimal for reporting of complaints were more urban places, advocacy as a primary orientation, and less familiarity with employees of facilities.

Urban advocates who did not know staff well reported an average of 3.05 complaints. Regardless of their role orientation, size of place, and whether they knew nursing home staff well, all other combinations of groups of volunteers reported substantially fewer complaints (ranging from .93 to 1.44) than urban advocates with no staff ties, and they did not differ from one another in the number of reported complaints.

SUMMARY AND IMPLICATIONS

This analysis makes a contribution by linking community size, volunteers' role orientations, and the nature of their social ties with facility staff and residents to their activities on behalf of nursing home residents. By using data from individual volunteers and an independent measure of their complaint reports from organizational records, the research provides a view of how review of care in nursing facilities may differ in rural and urban areas. Moreover, very small communities that have been excluded in some earlier research were considered.

One objective of ombudsman programs is to enhance advocacy skills among volunteers (Harris-Wehling et al., 1995). Anticipated difficulties with reporting complaints expressed by volunteers in their applications and reported in chapter 4 illustrate why an orientation toward advocacy and its accompanying skills may be difficult to acquire and maintain. For example, volunteers commented: "Confrontation is a problem for me," The most difficult thing would be "to be aggressive or argumentative to improve situations," "Probably the most difficult thing for me would be to take a bold stand in order to protect a patient's rights," "To be properly critical of the caring of others will be hardest." These expressions of difficulty did not even broach the additional strain that might occur in the evaluation of the performance of an acquaintance or friend.

Rural volunteers less often acted on the identity of advocate when they espoused it. A lingering question then is why identification as an advocate and the absence of informal ties with facility personnel among rural volunteers failed to result in increased reports of complaints as they had among urban volunteers. Beyond the care they provide, there are reasons that different roles occupied by nursing facilities in rural and urban communities may influence the outcomes of volunteers' efforts in ombudsman programs even when they have no personal ties with facility staff.

Values and social relationships found in rural areas (Rowles, 1996) may shape decisions of volunteers despite their unfamiliarity with the facility and may override their predisposition to advocacy. Multiple, dense (overlapping) social ties and personalization may be more characteristic of rural than urban areas.

Dense social ties among community members may have a long reach. Rural values may permeate the relationship between nursing facilities and their communities independent of whether individual volunteers know facility employees and residents. Rural volunteers, regardless of their orientation toward their work and informal ties with the facility, may be embedded in community expectations that do not endorse whistle blowing to the same extent as in larger places. Consequently, practicing advocacy that may involve being critical of fellow citizens may be more disjunctive with rural values. Thus, the very advantage of potentially closer relationships between rural communities and their nursing homes (Rowles, 1996) may be somewhat detrimental for those who would practice advocacy and for recipients of their efforts.

These findings have implications for recruitment of volunteers to serve in nursing facilities, especially in rural places. It may be more difficult to recruit rural volunteers because of physical distance (Netting & Hinds, 1989). In communities with disproportionately older populations, there also may be smaller pools of persons from which to select advocates.

Although a preference is for volunteers who do not know residents (Schiman & Lordeman, 1989) and facility employees, it is less likely that rural volunteers will be unfamiliar with the facility. Furthermore, familiarity with employees, residents, the facility, and its place in the community often are major reasons for volunteering. Motivations to volunteer independent of informal ties or psychological investment in the facility may need to be enhanced. If the pool of volunteers is to include those familiar with the facility and its personnel, training will be needed in interviewing, investigating, and reporting complaints under these circumstances. As volunteers open nursing homes to communities (Nelson, 1995), the need for instruction will be accentuated in rural areas. Finally, if the objective is to increase advocacy rather than providing primarily psychological support and friendship, it will be difficult to shift rewards obtained from friendly visiting to those received from an often more circuitous route of aggressive advocacy. Volunteers' benefits from advocacy may sometimes be less apparent and deferred.

Substantially fewer individuals initially volunteer for the rewards from advocacy than for the personal satisfaction obtained from cheering, visiting, and serving as companions to residents. It should be noted that friendly visitors performed similarly (i.e., reported complaints) regardless of community size or social relationships with facility employees and residents. To trade off friendly visiting and its rewards for serious advocacy may enhance possibilities for stress and conflict, and such circumstances may be especially inhospitable for rural volunteers where there is high integration of facilities and the community.

Contrary to the caution against placing volunteers in ombudsman programs in facilities in which they have friends and relatives, a potentially positive feature of the findings was that informal ties between volunteers and residents seemed benign and did not intrude on or thwart the work of the former. Although attitudes of residents and assistance from them are important in carrying out activities in ombudsman programs (Nelson, 1995), opposition from nursing facility staff is one of the most discouraging factors (Litwin & Monk, 1984). It was perhaps this potential opposition from administrators and staff that was tempered by informal ties, which, in turn, limited reported complaints. Close social relationships with residents likely will not threaten the complaint process in the same way as will those with staff members.

CONCLUSION

In summary, if active advocacy (i.e., increased reports of complaints) is a primary objective for volunteers in both rural and urban ombudsman programs, somewhat ironic sets of circumstances must be taken into account in training and programming. First, the role orientation of the majority of volunteers (visiting, companionship) did not facilitate active advocacy in large or small communities. To maximize advocacy, many persons will need to change not only their practices but also their identity as volunteers.

Paradoxically, greater integration of rural facilities and their communities, a benefit in other situations, may hamper the complaint process among volunteers who identify with advocacy and otherwise might file complaints. A benefit of volunteering may be the formation of group ties that become "psychosocial resources" for participants (Van Willigen, 2000). This research suggests that a potential benefit for volunteers in some instances may disadvantage those whom they serve. Finding ways to turn these circumstances, some of which initially attract persons to what has been called the most difficult job in the field of aging, into a context wherein advocacy can thrive must be undertaken in communities of all sizes. But practitioners and organizations in smaller places, where needs of elders and volunteers may be proportionally greater, will encounter some of the most significant challenges.

Chapter 8

Role Orientations, Attributions to Nursing Facility Personnel, and Unresolved Complaints of Volunteers

This chapter continues the study of role orientations by focusing on the nature of volunteers' relationships with nursing facility personnel and unresolved complaints. Attribution of hindrances specifically to facility personnel and lack of support from them, perceived effectiveness in managing administrative complaints, and orientation of volunteers were considered in relation to unresolved complaints. I also investigated the extent to which attributions to facility staff, perceptions of effectiveness in resolving administrative complaints, and unresolved complaints differentiated among role orientations of volunteers. In chapters 5 and 6, a global measure of hindrances from nine sources was considered; in this chapter, only specific hindrances attributed to facility staff were studied in relation to the management of complaints.

RELATED LITERATURE

The nursing facility is the primary setting for the work of many volunteers in ombudsman programs. Yet volunteers' perceptions of their relationship to nursing facility personnel in their work in ombudsman programs are not often studied. Administrators and their staff, however, may facilitate, thwart, or be ambivalent toward the efforts of volunteers who function in the facility. This research linked volunteers' orientations to their work, their perceptions of attitudes and hindering behavior of facility personnel, and unresolved complaints. Unresolved complaints are one objective measure of the work of volunteers.

A portion of chapter 8 was published in P. Keith, (2001), "Role Orientations, Attributions to Nursing Facility Personnel and Unresolved Complaints of Volunteers in an Ombudsman Program," *Journal of Gerontological Social Work* 26:249–260.

Measures of volunteers' work are often not considered in relation to their views of their work or their relationships with and support from facility personnel.

Orientations of volunteers to their work reflect primary functions of ombudsman programs. Evans (1996) observed that the approach of ombudsmen is frequently differential and individualized, and they take on varied roles. As noted in earlier chapters, orientations of volunteers may include those of advocate, therapeutic supporter (friendly visitor), mediator, and educator (Harris-Wehling et al., 1995; Monk et al., 1984). In turn, there is a suggested connection between orientations of volunteers and how they may be regarded by facility staff. For example, Netting et al. (1995, p. 355) observed, "The roles performed by ombudsmen are not always appreciated in their communities. Depending on the relationship between long-term care administrators ... and staff members of the local program, an ombudsman may be perceived as a watchdog to be avoided, a friendly visitor to be tolerated, or a resource for advice and assistance." Even though the volunteers in this research were referred to as resident advocates rather than ombudsmen, effects of attitudes toward their roles by staff of nursing facilities may be similar to their perceptions of ombudsmen.

Whether they are avoided, tolerated, or used as a resource may depend in part on the volunteers' primary orientation and their practices. There is some evidence in the literature that volunteers who practice advocacy to a greater extent than do friendly visitors may experience greater strain and conflict in the work setting (Monk et al., 1984). Monk et al. (1984) observed that nursing facility staff highlighted the importance of the therapeutic model in contrast to their rejection of the advocate approach. That even ombudsmen tended to favor a more expressive, warmer approach suggests that their peers who focused primarily on advocacy may have occupied a more deviant position if not also one of greater stress. A volunteer's primary orientation of advocacy may differ substantially from both that of peers and that preferred by facility administrators and staff.

Some facility administrators who were questioned in one study believed that ombudsmen viewed their relationship with nursing facilities as adversarial (Lusky, Friedsam, & Ingman, 1994). "In some instances, it was clear that any involvement of the ombudsman beyond mediation and limited advocacy was seen as an intrusion on the staff's professional responsibility and as a challenge to staff authority" (Lusky et al., 1994, p. 9). The approach of those who identify primarily with advocacy may reflect the most deviant views among volunteers in some ombudsman programs, and conceptions of their primary tasks may be most out of favor with those of nursing facility administrators and their staff. In turn, the latter may hinder the work of advocates most.

This situation suggests that volunteers in an ombudsman program who perform in a way most congruent with preferences of facility staff likely will view the latter as more positive and supportive. If facility staff are viewed by volunteers as barriers or hindrances to effective performance of their activities, this attitude also may be reflected in a more objective indicator of their efforts such as management of complaints. Hindrances by facility personnel may limit resolution of complaints. When reporting and resolving complaints are expected volunteer activities, a greater magnitude of unresolved complaints may represent less success and a lower-quality performance than might be possible with greater support from staff and administrators.

The reasoning was that a larger number of unresolved complaints would indicate the presence of more stressful circumstances for volunteers than if fewer remained unresolved. If views attributed to administrators and staff were important to the work of volunteers, then the former should be linked with measures of the efforts of advocates. Unresolved complaints may reflect lingering problems that seem to recur or are sustained despite efforts to solve them. For example, one volunteer commented, "I am very troubled by complaints that we report and report and report only to find they are never resolved. This is stressful." To the extent that reporting and resolving complaints are more salient to volunteers with advocacy as a primary orientation, a lack of support attributed to facility staff may be more closely associated with unresolved complaints among persons who identify with advocacy than among those with other orientations.

Based on the literature, a first objective was to investigate the relationship between primary orientations of volunteers toward their tasks and the views they attributed to facility personnel. Did attitudes and actions attributed to facility personnel differ by primary orientations of volunteers or were staff seen as equally supportive regardless of the primary orientation and practices of the volunteer? A further objective was to consider volunteers' primary orientations, perceived effectiveness, and the views attributed to facility staff in relation to the amount of unresolved complaints.

HYPOTHESES

Drawing on the limited available literature, I formulated two hypotheses.

1. Specific attribution of greater hindrances and negative attitudes to facility personnel, perception of less effectiveness in resolving complaints about administrative practices, and more unresolved complaints differentiate advocates from two other orientations, that is, mediators and therapeutic supporters. Advocates attribute more hindrances and negative attitudes to facility personnel, feel less effective in resolving complaints about administrative practices, and serve on committees with more unresolved complaints than do persons with other orientations.

2. Attribution of greater hindrances and negative attitudes to facility personnel and perception of less effectiveness in resolving administrative complaints are associated with more unresolved complaints.

MEASURES

Volunteers' Orientations

In this chapter, volunteers who identified one of the three general types of orientations (advocate, mediator, or therapeutic supporter) were included in the analyses. The procedure used to determine the primary orientation of volunteers is described in chapter 6. Individuals who did not distinguish a primary orientation were excluded from the analyses in this chapter.

Attributions to Nursing Facility Personnel

Volunteers assessed nursing facility staffs' (administrators' and aides') perceptions of the work of the resident advocates using a semantic differential format with four polar adjectives on a seven-point scale (1–7, important-unimportant, unfair-fair, needed-not needed, ineffective-effective). Responses were summed across the four adjectives to form two separate scales for attributions of perceptions to administrators and aides (alpha, .84, .84, respectively). A higher score reflected more positive attitudes (table 8.1).

Volunteers noted how often they felt hindered in their work by "Resistance by the facility administrator" and "Resistance by other staff in the facility" ("Never" [1] to "Very often" [5]). The items were analyzed separately, and a higher score indicated greater hindrances (table 8.1). Finally, in response to a single item, volunteers rated their effectiveness in handling complaints about nursing facility administration ("Not effective at all" [1] to "Very effective" [5]).

Unresolved Complaints

The number of complaints and resolutions recorded in quarterly reports over a two-year period were collected from records on-site at eight Area Agencies on Aging. Reports ($n = 1,886$) for a two-year period were coded. Complaints and resolutions were each summed, and the total number of resolutions were subtracted from the total number of complaints to obtain the number of unresolved complaints. I thought that a larger amount of unresolved, sometimes lingering, complaints would be more stressful for volunteers than fewer unresolved issues.

ANALYSES

A reduced sample was used in these analyses to study unresolved complaints. Only respondents who had made quarterly reports of their activities, who had filed some complaints, and who identified a primary role orientation were included in the calculation of unresolved complaints ($n = 481$).

Table 8.1

One-Way Analyses of Variance of Volunteers' Role Orientations by Their Attributions to Facility Personnel, Effectiveness, and Unresolved Complaints

	Advocate $\bar{x}$	Mediator $\bar{x}$	Therapeutic Supporter $\bar{x}$	sd	F	p
Attitudes Attributed to Facility Administrators	21.28	21.38	22.70	5.47	8.07	.001
Attitudes Attributed to Facility Aides	19.16	19.84	21.36	5.41	10.87	.001
Hindrances from Facility Administrators	1.74	1.41	1.36	.90	3.23	.05
Hindrances from Facility Aides	1.75	1.44	1.35	.80	6.89	.001
Effectiveness in Managing Administrative Complaints	3.58	3.68	3.80	.86	3.12	.05
Number of Unresolved Complaints	8.69	6.91	5.18	10.36	5.20	.01

Discriminant analysis was used to test the hypotheses, and one-way analyses of variance amplified the findings. Demographic characteristics (e.g., age, gender, education) were largely unrelated to volunteers' attributions to administrators and staff, perceptions of their own effectiveness in handling administrative complaints, or the amount of unresolved complaints and were not included in the hypotheses or analyses.

RESULTS

Bivariate Analyses

Volunteers in this subsample identified their primary orientations: advocate, 27 percent; mediator, 15 percent; and therapeutic supporter (friendly visitor), 58 percent. In one-way analyses of variance, the three orientations of volunteers to their work in the ombudsman program were considered in relation to their attributions to facility personnel, assessment of their own effectiveness in resolving administrative complaints, and the amount of unresolved complaints.

Bivariate analyses showed that advocates attributed more negative attitudes to facility personnel than did therapeutic supporters (table 8.1). Attributions made by mediators were located between those of the other two groups. Advocates experienced greater hindrances from both administrators and facility staff than did mediators and therapeutic supporters, and they rated their effectiveness in resolving complaints about administrative practices significantly lower than did therapeutic supporters.

Advocates served on committees with more unresolved complaints than those of volunteers who were predominantly friendly visitors (table 8.1). The average number of unresolved complaints of mediators was located between those of the other two groups and did not differ significantly from either of them.

Multivariate Analyses

Orientations of Volunteers

The first hypothesis was that more negative attributions to facility personnel, perceptions of ineffectiveness, and unresolved complaints differentiated advocates from other orientations. To test the hypothesis, six variables were considered simultaneously in a discriminant analysis of the typology of three primary orientations of volunteers. The variables included were hindrances attributed to administrators and aides, attitudes of facility administration and staff toward the work of volunteers, effectiveness in resolving complaints about administration, and number of unresolved complaints (table 8.2). In the discriminant analysis, there was one significant function ($\chi^2 = 37.33$, $p < .001$). When all variables were considered together, of the characteristics attributed to facility personnel, attitudes of personnel toward the work of volunteers were among the most important variables in differentiating advocates from the other two groups (table 8.2). Advocates who found the attitudes of facility personnel most negative differed from the other two groups. A larger number of unresolved complaints distinguished advocates from other orientations. Although the coefficient was smaller than for the other variables, greater hindrances attributed to administrators also differentiated advocates from mediators and friendly visitors. Examination of the canonical discriminant functions at the group means (group centroids) indicated the advocates were located farthest (.51) from the friendly visitors (−.22), with mediators in between (−.01). Those who provided psychological support and mediation were most similar.

The first hypothesis was only partially supported. Although hindrances attributed to aides and negative perceptions of their own effectiveness were significantly related to orientations of volunteers at the bivariate level, they were not very salient in the multivariate analysis.

Unresolved Complaints

The hypothesis that volunteers' attributions to facility personnel would be associated with the amount of unresolved complaints was tested using regres-

Table 8.2

Discriminant Analysis of Attributions to Nursing Facility Personnel,
Effectiveness, and Unresolved Complaints by Role Orientations of Volunteers

	Role Orientations of Volunteers
	(Standardized Discriminant Function Coefficients)
Attitudes Attributed to Facility Administrators	.47
Attitudes Attributed to Facility Aides	.53
Hindrances from Facility Administrators	.38
Hindrances from Facility Aides	.28
Effectiveness in Managing Administrative Complaints	.25
Number of Unresolved Complaints	.51
Canonical Correlation	.30
χ^2 (df = 12; p<.001)	37.33

sion analysis. Analyses were conducted separately for each of the three types of orientations. The five variables, including attitudes toward the work of volunteers, hindrances attributed to facility personnel, and volunteers' perceptions of their own effectiveness, were considered in relation to the amount of unresolved complaints.

Three of the variables explained 18 percent of the variance in unresolved complaints among advocates. Negative attitudes toward the ombudsman program attributed to administrators ($b = -.55, t = 3.48, p < .001$), hindrances from aides ($b = .33, t = 2.02, p < .05$), and perceptions of their own ineffectiveness in resolving administrative complaints ($b = .26, t = 2.22, p < .05$) were associated with more unresolved complaints among advocates. Although perceived administrative support for the program directly influenced unresolved complaints, its effect was also mediated through volunteers' belief about their effectiveness in resolving administrative complaints. In contrast, none of the five variables including volunteers' attributions to facility personnel and assessment of their own effectiveness explained a significant amount of variance in unresolved complaints among mediators and friendly visitors. Therefore, the second hypothesis was partially supported, and only among advocates.

Consequently, volunteers who identified advocacy as their primary orientation to their work with residents tended to have different experiences with facility personnel and viewed their own effectiveness differently. And these experiences tended to be associated with the outcomes of their work.

DISCUSSION

In this chapter, I investigated the extent to which attributions to facility staff varied by primary orientations of volunteers and were related to unresolved complaints filed on behalf of residents. Volunteers assessed the extent to which nursing facility staff were favorable toward the ombudsman program or hindered their efforts. A significant feature of the analysis was linking volunteers' attitudes with an objective indicator of their practices.

The potential for animosity toward volunteer participants in an ombudsman program may be greater than for other types of volunteering (Nathanson & Eggleton, 1993). Compared with volunteers with a primary orientation toward friendly visitor, volunteers who had a primary orientation toward advocacy had relationships with facility personnel that were considerably more negative.

Some of the explanation for the divergent perceptions of volunteers in ombudsman programs more generally may be found in their disparate views of nursing facility staff. One perspective is that ombudsmen are typically seen as an adversary by facility personnel (Evans, 1996). Another view suggests that the primary orientation of volunteers may in part determine how they are received, with that of advocate being the least favored and the most threatening (Netting et al., 1995). Still other research has not found uniform approval of even the potentially less adversarial orientations (Lusky et al., 1994). There is, for example, some evidence that "companionship and caring activities," closely akin to the "therapeutic supporter" approach, were not rated as "very important" by administrators uniformly across a sample of states. Respondents in smaller facilities, more often than persons in larger ones, identified "enriching the lives of residents through companionship and caring" as important, and they more frequently viewed "providing companionship and social support to residents" as a primary or secondary function of the program (Lusky et al., 1994).

Observing, receiving, and reporting complaints in a persistent manner were accompanied by the feeling among volunteers that facility personnel may have seen the former's work as less important, unneeded, unfair, and ineffective. Some of these same facility personnel were seen as hindrances to the work of volunteers. Advocates most often reported more complaints and also functioned with the burden of more unresolved concerns of residents. It is unlikely that volunteers who identified as advocates were more active in reporting complaints just by chance or were necessarily located in facilities with more difficulties. They were acting on their views of advocacy as a primary function of volunteers who were a part of an ombudsman program. Furthermore, reports of complaints and attempts to resolve them likely would increase interaction with facility administrators and their staff. Thwarted resolutions may have culminated in some advocates' views that facility staff were negative toward the ombudsman program and sometimes hindered their efforts. The majority of volunteers in this research identified with the "therapeutic supportive" stance and described their primary activities as friendly visitors. Correspondingly, these volunteers filed fewer complaints. If filing more complaints was seen as adversarial, then the behavior of advocates was perhaps more confrontational than that of other patterns. A larger number of unresolved complaints may have reflected numerous attempts to obtain a solution, as reflected in the comment, "We have to go back and ask and ask about the same problems and still they are not taken care of."

A further indication that the climate for advocates contrasts with that of other volunteers was that attributions to staff and perceptions of effectiveness in resolving administrative complaints were independent of the number of unresolved complaints of mediators and friendly visitors. Whatever mediators and friendly visitors may have thought about the supportiveness of facility staff or the nature of their experiences was immaterial to their success or failure in resolving the complaints as measured in this research. For advocates, the hindrances and attitudes attributed to staff figured prominently in how they managed their work. Insofar as deliberations involve conflict over complaints and their resolution, relationships between advocates and facility personnel likely had more opportunity to deteriorate. This may especially have been the case where complaints were made repeatedly without being addressed by administration.

Because the orientation of some volunteers was associated with their views of the climate in which they practiced and the outcomes of their work (e.g., unresolved complaints), those who recruit and train persons who serve in ombudsman programs may want to remember the importance of ideology to volunteers. There is a need for instruction in skills of advocacy and in managing the complaint process among volunteers regardless of their primary orientation. Greater emphasis on advocacy in training may aid those with a focus on friendly visiting to expand their skills. For volunteers who already primarily practice advocacy and try to bring about change in residents' circumstances, training may enable them to handle complaints more effectively and to assist peer volunteers who have fewer skills.

Increased concerns about quality of life in general, including the quality of long-term care for residents, suggest needs for further investigation (Arcus, 1999). Recently, Nelson (2000) described a climate of injustice and conflict in nursing facilities in which a structure of dependence and control precludes fair bargaining by residents and staff. A remaining question concerns the extent to which strong advocates may decrease inequities experienced in nursing facilities and establish a balance of power. A task of future research may be to link features of the organizational climate of nursing facilities, indicators of quality of care as defined by residents, an assessment of the specific long-term care ombudsman program, and the work of volunteers (Huber, Borders, Badrak, Netting, & Nelson, 2001). The need for increased attention to residents as recipients of the efforts of volunteers is highlighted by research that demonstrated the importance of collecting data on demographic characteristics of residents in relation to complaints and their resolution (Huber, Borders, Netting, & Nelson, 2001). Finally, volunteers' quality of life should be studied further in relation to the administrative, staff, and resident climate in the nursing facilities in which they review and advocate for improved care.

Chapter 9

Support from Others and Efficacy of Volunteers

SUPPORT AND EFFICACY

There is general literature on the importance of support for volunteers, but there has been less systematic research linking support received and efficacy of volunteers. In this chapter, I assess the relative contribution of peers, family, residents, nursing facility staff, and aging network personnel to feelings of efficacy among volunteers in the ombudsman program. This chapter extends research about volunteers and the relative importance of sources of support for their feelings of efficacy. It is important to study efficacy of volunteers because those who feel most competent are most likely to persist and be most satisfied (Fischer & Schaffer, 1993). Indeed, reduced efficacy or accomplishment is a component of burnout (Maslach et al., 2001). Efficacy reflects the exercise of control. It indicates the extent to which persons believe they may control the direction of their behavior. Individuals seek to maintain control over areas that are viewed as improvable (Bandura, 1997). Review of care and, if possible, improvement of the circumstances of residents were among the tasks of these volunteers.

Social support is most often thought of and studied as a buffer from difficulties in life (Bandura, 1997). But support is more than this and affects patterns of activity by increasing beliefs of personal efficacy. This research investigated the enabling function of support that increases perceived coping efficacy (Major et al., 1990). To enhance efficacy, persons draw on others for support and assis-

A portion of chapter 9 was published in P. Keith, (2001), "Support from Others and Efficacy of Volunteer Ombudsmen in Long Term Care Facilities," *International Journal of Aging and Human Development*, Volume 52, Number 4, pp. 297–310, Baywood Publishing Company, Inc., Amityville, N.Y.

tance. The contributions of support to feelings of efficacy have been established in several areas, for example, among family members (Gross, Conrad, Fogg, & Wothke, 1994) and among the young and old (Bandura, 1997). The premise of the hypotheses tested here about support and efficacy is that "[a]cquaintances model coping attitudes and skills, provide incentives for engagement in beneficial activities, and motivate others by showing that difficulties are surmountable by perseverant effort" (Bandura, 1997, p. 206). These processes should operate among volunteers and emphasize the importance their behavior may have for one another. In one study, volunteers identified a support group and opportunities to know other volunteers well among their needs (Scott & Caldwell, 1996).

Fellow volunteers who are committed, have low turnover, and who maintain pleasant relationships should be good models and, as Bandura (1997) suggests, motivate one another. In these circumstances, volunteers could learn coping skills from one another. Commitment to the tasks of advocacy may provide incentives to others to engage in the activities and to persevere in difficult cases of residents' rights. Volunteers who function in these conditions with support from one another should have greater efficacy in their work. Most volunteers studied worked in committees that met regularly and provided an opportunity for interaction and mutual support.

In addition to assistance from volunteer peers with whom they serve, support from those who organize and coordinate efforts of volunteers also should be important. Support from an organization may take the form of education, training, and recognition of volunteer efforts (Scott & Caldwell, 1996). Volunteers who are cared for this way may experience greater feelings of mastery. In this chapter, I consider efficacy of volunteers in relation to perceptions of general support from a variety of persons rather than help derived from specific activities. In the next chapter, education and training, as illustrative of more specific types of support, are investigated in relation to efficacy and worry of volunteers.

The absence of organizational caring may be reflected in turnover, which is a frequent problem in maintaining programs that operate primarily with the help of volunteers (Fischer & Schaffer, 1993). Turnover may disrupt the support volunteers provide one another. To the extent that turnover is experienced as an interference, I expected that turnover of volunteer advocates would diminish the efficacy of those with whom they work.

A question in this chapter is whether relationships with and support from other volunteers facilitated efficacy more than assistance from family, residents, nursing facility staff, and those in the aging network. Many studies indicate that for one form of support—caregiving—actual involvement in sustained instrumental care forms a hierarchy from close family members to those more distant (see Atchley, 1997, for a review). Analyses in this chapter go a bit further to investigate which groups that provide support contribute most to feelings of efficacy as volunteers perform their activities.

Support from those in closest proximity to the site of the evaluation of residents' circumstances may contribute most to the work and subsequent efficacy of ombudsmen. Personnel, especially administrators, in care facilities have opportunities to create barriers or to facilitate the review of residents' conditions. Consequently, they are in critical positions to affect implementation of recommendations, resolution of complaints, and perhaps later feelings of efficacy. I based my hypotheses on these considerations and on literature indicating the possible significance of fellow volunteers for decisions to continue as volunteers (Scott & Caldwell, 1996) and the relationship between support and efficacy (Bandura, 1997).

Hypotheses

1. Support received from persons most closely affiliated with nursing facilities and in direct contact with the assessment process (residents, administrators, nurses, and aides) and from other volunteers in the ombudsman program enhances efficacy more than assistance from those who are in less close proximity to the tasks of volunteers (family members of both volunteers and residents, friends, or personnel in the aging network).

2. Maintenance of a good relationship with fellow volunteers, affiliation with more committed volunteers, and situations in which turnover does not interfere with work are associated with greater efficacy of volunteers in the ombudsman program.

3. Volunteers who believe their needs are taken into account and are not overlooked experience greater efficacy.

PROCEDURES

Measures

Support Received

Respondents indicated the amount of support they received from ten possible sources. They noted whether they had received "a great deal" (3), "some" (2), or "no" (1) support from the following: other volunteers in the ombudsman program, long-term care residents, residents' families, facility administrator, nursing staff, aides, resident advocate coordinator at the Area Agency on Aging, state ombudsman, family, and friends. Amounts of support received from the ten sources were used as separate indicators.

Volunteer Relationships and Needs

Using a five-point scale, volunteers strongly agreed (1) or strongly disagreed (5) with the following statements: volunteers with whom they worked were usually very committed to care review, good personal relationships with other volunteers were one reason why they continued to participate in the program, turnover of other volunteers made their work more difficult, and sometimes the needs of volunteers are overlooked.

Efficacy

Six items measured efficacy on a five-point scale ("Strongly agree" [1] to "Strongly disagree" [5]). Representative items were "Sometimes I feel I have little control over my activities," "I believe there are positive changes I can make in the lives of residents," and "I sometimes feel helpless in deciding how best to approach the problems and complaints of residents." The six items were summed. Data were coded so that a higher score reflected greater efficacy ($\bar{x} =$ 19.99, sd = 3.37, alpha = .67).

Analyses

Data were analyzed using percentages and correlations. Hypotheses were tested with multiple regression. To ease repetitiveness, the terms *support*, *assistance*, and *help* are used interchangeably. Fellow or peer volunteers and peers refer to volunteers in the ombudsman program with whom respondents worked.

RESULTS

Table 9.1 shows the extent to which volunteers received support from several sources with their tasks in the program. More than half of the volunteers (55 percent) obtained a great deal of assistance from administrators of nursing facilities. Administrators provided more help than any other group of persons. Fellow volunteers were one of the frequent providers of considerable support (47 percent). More than one-third of the volunteers received a great deal of assistance from some of the other groups, including nursing staff (43 percent), Area Agency on Aging volunteer coordinators (36 percent), family members (35 percent), and aides at the facilities (34 percent). About one-fifth of the remaining groups lent a great deal of support to a number of volunteers: residents (28 percent), state ombudsman (21 percent), residents' families (20 percent), and friends (20 percent). Other volunteers, however, observed that their families, friends, families of residents, and the state ombudsman provided no support.

Correlations among the variables are shown in table 9.2. Although attention to individual sources of assistance was the focus of this research, I calculated a scale for support based on sums of responses to the ten items ($\bar{x} = 21.79$, sd = 3.95, alpha = .81). A higher score reflected greater support. All sources of sup-

Table 9.1
Support Volunteers Received from Others

| | Support Received | | | | | |
| | A Great Deal | | Some | | None | |
Sources of Support	N	Percent	N	Percent	N	Percent
Volunteers	350	47.4	337	45.7	51	6.9
Residents	195	27.5	403	56.9	110	15.5
Administration	398	54.6	297	40.7	34	4.7
Nursing Staff	314	43.0	373	51.1	43	5.9
Aides	245	33.7	404	55.6	78	10.7
Residents Families	145	20.3	402	56.1	169	23.6
Family	252	35.4	281	39.5	178	25.0
Friends	140	19.7	359	50.6	210	29.6
Volunteer Coordinator	256	35.5	397	55.0	69	9.6
State Ombudsman	147	21.4	382	55.5	159	23.1

port were significantly related to one another (table 9.2). Among single items, only support from the state ombudsman was not related to efficacy. Overall support was significantly correlated with efficacy ($r = .26, p < .01$). However, this obscured individual items of interest that were not associated with efficacy in the multivariate analysis.

A multiple regression analysis was used to test the hypotheses. Amount of support from various sources, measures reflecting relationships among volunteers, and whether needs of volunteers were taken into account were included in the stepwise regression of volunteers' efficacy (table 9.3).

The first hypothesis—that assistance from persons most closely associated with the nursing facility and in closest proximity to where assessments of residents' conditions take place would contribute the most to volunteers efficacy— was only partially supported. Among facility personnel, only assistance received from administrators was associated with feelings of efficacy of volunteers when all variables were considered simultaneously. Support from residents also increased efficacy of volunteers, but assistance from nurses did not directly affect these feelings. Because of the strong relationship between volunteers' assessments of support of nurses and aides, only that of nurses was included in the final model of efficacy shown in table 9.3. However, when support

Table 9.2
Pearson Correlations among Support, Relationships with Other Volunteers, and Efficacy

Support and Relationships	1	2	3	4	5	6	7	8	9	10	11	12	13	14	15
1. Efficacy	1.000														
2. Volunteers	.073*	1.000													
3. Residents	.196**	.333**	1.000												
4. Administration	.328**	.281**	.194**	1.000											
5. Nursing Staff	.230**	.236**	.280**	.557**	1.000										
6. Aides	.191**	.249**	.309**	.412**	.673**	1.000									
7. Residents Families	.185**	.281**	.449**	.213**	.296**	.307**	1.000								
8. Family	.151**	.331**	.335**	.252**	.274**	.257**	.310**	1.000							
9. Friends	.106*	.304**	.400**	.202**	.239**	.247**	.364**	.537**	1.000						
10. Volunteer Coordinator	.119**	.322**	.219**	.239**	.246**	.186**	.215**	.261**	.198**	1.000					
11. State Ombudsman	.058	.254**	.256**	.179**	.221**	.280**	.260**	.234**	.258**	.464**	1.000				
12. Volunteer Needs Overlooked	.194**	.059	.032	.072	.029	.013	.017	.010	.006	-.030	-.023	1.000			
13. Volunteer Commitment	-.176**	-.257**	-.139**	-.223**	-.207**	-.162**	-.173**	-.176**	-.165**	-.167**	-.190**	-.080*	1.000		
14. Positive Relationships w/Volunteers	-.036	-.293**	-.156**	-.158**	-.155**	-.153**	-.177**	-.188**	-.241**	-.185**	-.195**	.120**	.416**	1.000	
15. Difficulty/Volunteer Turnovers	.157**	.135**	.106**	.153**	.181**	.164**	.140**	.141**	.146**	.084*	.076*	.259**	-.225**	-.142**	1.000

*$p < .05$
**$p < .01$

Table 9.3
Multiple Regression of Support, Relationships with Peers, and Efficacy of Volunteers[a]

Support and Relationships	Beta	Std. Deviation	t
Volunteer commitment	.10	.21	2.44**
Volunteer needs overlooked	.14	.14	3.64***
Support from administration	.63	.69	5.40***
Support from residents	.43	.54	4.25***
Support from other volunteers	-.10	-.24	2.22**
Support from administrators X support from residents	.54	.32	3.41***

[a]Only significant coefficients are presented.
**$p < .05$
***$p < .01$

attributed to aides was considered in a separate regression analysis (not shown), it also was not significant in the multivariate model.

Although volunteers are not a part of the facility, much of their work takes place within it. Fellow volunteers may work closely with one another on assessments of resident care and may frequent the facility often. In contrast to the hypothesis, support received from volunteer peers was negatively associated with their efficacy when it was considered simultaneously with other variables in the model.

Among purveyors of support that contributed to efficacy, there was one significant interaction effect. The significant interaction effect between support from facility administrators and that from residents indicated that volunteer efficacy was lowest when there was no assistance from the administrator regardless of the amount of help received from residents ($F = 3.59, p < .01$). There were no significant two- or three-way interaction effects between support from fellow volunteers and that from administrators and residents.

The second hypothesis—that positive outcomes of affiliation with volunteer colleagues enhances efficacy—was partially confirmed. Committed fellow volunteers prompted individual efficacy, but neither good relationships with one another nor turnover affected how well volunteers believed they performed their activities. Confirming the final hypothesis, volunteers who felt cared for in the sense that their needs were taken into account viewed their work for the ombudsman program more positively.

One of the groups that provided the most support was among those who also contributed most to volunteers' efficacy. Administrators of facilities gave considerable assistance that enhanced volunteers' assessment of their efforts. In contrast, fellow volunteers who provided much support negatively affected their peers' feelings of efficacy. Nurses, aides, family members, and the volunteer coordinators contributed more assistance than some others, but this support was not reflected in volunteers' assessments of their own efficacy.

SUMMARY AND DISCUSSION

Outcomes of hypotheses about the importance of support and relationships with fellow volunteers for efficacy were mixed. Support provided by two of the five groups of persons in close contact with the assessment of residents' circumstances, including residents themselves, contributed most substantially to the efficacy of volunteers.

Assistance of long-term care administrators was crucial to volunteer efficacy and was one of its most important correlates. The administrator is in a position to highlight the efforts of the volunteers, indicate to other staff the importance of volunteers' activities, follow up on complaints, and implement recommendations. Assistance from other facility personnel was not reflected in volunteer efficacy. Beyond the direct contribution of administrators' support to volunteer efficacy, they also may have an opportunity to serve as models in their facilities for nurses and aides. Indeed, the positive correlations between support from nurses and aides and efficacy of volunteers disappeared when assistance from the administrator was controlled. A supportive atmosphere for the conduct of advocates' activities established by an administrator may have mediated the effects of assistance from other facility staff on volunteer efficacy.

A further reason administrative support rather than that of other staff was more salient to volunteer efficacy may be that there is less continuity in assistance from nurses and especially aides. The tenure of some volunteers far exceeded that of facility personnel. Research (Wacker, Roberto, & Piper, 1998) and reports from minutes of meetings of volunteers studied indicate that staff turnover and shortage in nursing facilities is quite prevalent.

Interrupted and less-sustained support may lead to frequent negotiation between volunteers and facility staff. The need to establish and reestablish legitimacy for an activity that may be threatening to some staff, especially those with the least training, may erode volunteers' feelings of efficacy. The need for volunteers to establish relationships with new staff who have significant resident contact, and whose actions are among the most frequently evaluated, may contribute little to volunteer efficacy.

Commitment to an activity suggests the importance that activity has for persons, and commitment and efficacy are linked (Singer & Coffin, 1996). Among workers, commitment to an organization may be a more important factor in turnover than job satisfaction (see Singh & Schwab, 1998, for a review). Commitment to an activity may be even more salient to efficacy and retention of volunteers, who do not have wage and benefit incentives. A high level of commitment may allow ombudsmen to persevere despite circumstances in a facility that might drive the less dedicated away. This research tested whether commitment among fellow volunteers enhanced the efficacy of their associates (Bandura, 1997).

That affiliation with more-committed peers fostered feelings of control among volunteers and was a source of support in itself was indicated in several ways. For example, volunteers whose good personal relationships were a factor in their continued volunteering were surrounded with more-committed peers ($r = .42, p < .001$). Turnover was less often experienced negatively when peer volunteers were highly committed ($r = .22, p < .001$). Committed colleagues may buffer the problems of turnover for one another as well as likely reduce the occurrence of turnover.

In other research, needs identified most frequently by highly effective volunteers included having a volunteer support group and opportunities to get to know other volunteers better (Scott & Caldwell, 1996). In the present research, however, the quality of volunteers' affiliation with coworkers did not directly increase efficacy. Rather, opportunities to affiliate with and perhaps model committed peers enhanced feelings of success as ombudsmen. Just as characteristics of volunteers may differentiate the kinds of positions they fill (Okun & Eisenberg, 1992), the type of volunteering—whether task oriented or primarily focused on social functions—may be a factor in the importance that social relationships with fellow volunteers has for volunteers' efficacy. Commitment of volunteer peers to their work, more than friendly social relationships, facilitated the perception of a job well done.

Another source of support of volunteers was feeling that their needs were recognized and taken into account. Literature suggests the importance of caring for volunteers through training, follow-up, and recognition for service (Duncan, 1995). When volunteers believed that their needs were considered, their efficacy increased.

A significant interaction effect demonstrated again the salience of the support provided by facility administrators and the fate of help from residents. When administrators did not support the work of the ombudsman program, even a great deal of assistance by residents failed to increase efficacy of volunteers.

One kind of support from residents likely takes the form of willingness and ability to communicate with the visiting volunteer. One of the difficulties in assisting older persons in long-term care facilities is the inability of residents to indicate their preferences or to describe their circumstances. Guardians of the least-competent older people, for example, also identified the inability to communicate with their wards to be among their hardest tasks (Keith & Wacker,

1994). Close to one-fifth of the volunteers studied mentioned communication as the most difficult aspect of their activities in the care facility.

Much support provided to volunteers was benign in its effect on their efficacy. A somewhat counterintuitive finding was that receiving a great deal of assistance from fellow volunteers had a negative effect on efficacy. Both positive and negative effects of receiving support, however, have been documented (Antonucci, Sherman, & Akiyama, 1996). Some of the contrast in outcomes of support from administrators, residents, and fellow volunteers may be attributable to differences in what they provide.

Residents offer information on their circumstances and how they are cared for; administrators are in a position to respond to complaints, ease the work of volunteers, and increase accessibility of the facility. Peer volunteers may observe one another, differ in their assessments, and experience conflict with one another's judgments about whether or how to report an observation. In such a context, failed support may occur (Antonucci et al., 1996). Accomplishment of the very activities that might foster feelings of efficacy may be thwarted somewhat by the intrusiveness of needed or unneeded assistance from peers. Volunteers may feel vulnerable in their efforts to care (Dancy & Wynn-Dancy, 1995).

Another explanation for the negative relationship between support from fellow volunteers and efficacy is that the assistance may not have been very good. Well-intended assistance from a poorly trained peer may be a negative feature of limited support. It also may be that volunteers with more problems demand more support from their peers, and they may experience a lack of efficacy despite more help from others. In chapter 5, hindrances attributed to poor training of peers were associated with volunteers' less-positive assessments of several of their experiences.

IMPLICATIONS

Clearly, among persons in the care facilities, administrators and residents were linchpins in aiding the efficacy of volunteers. It would be helpful to know more about the nature of support given by all groups, including the frequent assistance of nurses and aides, which did not directly affect the efficacy of volunteers.

It is important to remember that the data reported here are based on volunteers' subjective judgments. Information about their actual contact with residents, fellow volunteers, and other potential sources of support is not presented. Links between support and more objective measures of success in filing complaints are analyzed in chapter 5.

More needs to be known about how effectiveness of volunteers that may result in increased complaints influences their relationships with facility administrators. Future research should address whether early identification of problems by volunteers increases the support from administrators or dampens it and whether particular types of complaints (e.g., resident care, staff or administrative) result in differential support from administrators.

Even with the limitations noted, the research reinforces the importance of recognizing and attending to volunteers' needs. Located in Area Agencies on Aging, the coordinators of volunteers often are responsible for initial training and for providing in-service opportunities. Support from coordinators likely indirectly influenced the assistance fellow volunteers could offer one another. The research suggests that a part of the attention to volunteers should include building commitment to the tasks and to each other. Highly committed volunteers diminished the negative effects of turnover. Manifesting commitment to volunteer roles that have expectations for performance of instrumental tasks was more important than friendly social relationships among volunteers in ensuring feelings of efficacy. These outcomes, along with help from administrators and residents, were among the major pathways to efficacy for these volunteers.

Chapter 10

Training and Education Activities, Efficacy, and Worry among Volunteers

Threaded through the literature on volunteerism by and for older persons is the importance of training older volunteers. Training is believed to be correlated with a number of significant outcomes of volunteer participation including recruitment, retention, quality of performance, personal rewards, and psychological factors (Caro & Bass, 1995; Monk et al., 1984). Yet in a survey of literature on older volunteers covering more than a decade, only 13 of 393 annotated references were indexed as containing information on training (Bull & Levine, 1993).

Extending research on training and education of volunteers, this chapter has three objectives: investigation of (1) the extent to which preferences for education and training in specific areas and actual training were associated with assessment of training obtained prior to assuming volunteer tasks; (2) the extent to which preferences for education and training, assessment of training, and actual training were determinants of efficacy of volunteers; and (3) the relationship between preferences for education and training, assessment of training, actual training, and efficacy with worry about performing volunteer tasks. In addition, this chapter identifies the preferences of volunteers for eight types of training and education.

OUTCOMES OF TRAINING AND EDUCATION

Care and support from persons who organize and coordinate the efforts of volunteers are important for outcomes of volunteers. Care of volunteers may

A portion of chapter 10 was published in P. Keith, (2000), "Training/Education Activities, Efficacy, and Worry among Volunteer Ombudsmen in Nursing Facilities," *Journal of Educational Gerontology* 26:249–260. Permission to reprint has been granted by the publisher, Taylor & Francis Company.

include education, training, and recognition of their achievements (Scott & Caldwell, 1996). Support for volunteers reflected in education and training provides benefits to the organizations in which they work as well as to the individual volunteers.

Caro and Bass (1995, p. 88) observed that "[o]rganizations may improve the productivity of older volunteers through greater emphasis on training." As part of their research, volunteers indicated whether they received training and its adequacy for their major volunteer assignment. Most trained volunteers found that their training was adequate (97 percent). Among those with no training, some believed training would have helped a great deal (12 percent), would have made them more effective (15 percent), or would have benefited them in some way (20 percent). Training is differentiated among various kinds of volunteering.

Volunteer activities vary considerably in the skills and knowledge needed to perform them effectively. Characteristics of the work of volunteers in ombudsman programs suggest the special significance that training and educational opportunities may have for these volunteers. As noted in chapter 1, the roles of volunteers in ombudsman programs may be the most difficult in the field of aging (Monk et al., 1984).

The quality of training is salient in both recruitment and retention (Monk et al., 1984). One study of state ombudsmen concluded that quality of training was the second most important factor in recruitment, preceded by altruism of volunteers (Monk et al., 1984). Quality of training was the second most important factor in retention, following supervisory assistance. Training and education of volunteers contribute not only to the work of the organization but also to individuals' well-being and efforts.

Stebbins (1996) describes serious leisure volunteering as career volunteering. For such volunteering, acquisition of skills, knowledge, or training are required, and acquiring them is "highly rewarding." For career volunteering, the skills and knowledge needed are "substantial enough to engender a career built on their acquisition and on the difficult process of applying them" (Stebbins, 1996, p. 216). The observations and decisions made by volunteers in ombudsman programs may exemplify the sometimes difficult process of applying skills and knowledge, some of which are acquired through training. The direct outcomes of training for the well-being of individual volunteers is less-often documented than the significance of the activity of volunteering itself for participants.

VOLUNTARY ACTIVITY AND WELL-BEING

With some exceptions (see Turner, 1992), the link between voluntary activities and well-being has been established (Van Willigen, 2000). The benefits of volunteering for older persons, for example, was documented in a recent meta-analysis of thirty-seven studies (Wheeler, Gorey, & Greenblatt, 1998). Almost 75 percent of the volunteers scored higher on quality-of-life measures than did the typical nonparticipating counterparts, and the effects were sustained when health and socioeconomic status were controlled. In turn, 90 percent of the persons whom volunteers served also benefited.

Involvement in service-oriented organizations fosters feelings of control over life outcomes (Van Willigen, 1997). Hence, voluntarism increases feelings of efficacy. Indeed, voluntary work had a greater effect on well-being than any other social role, that is, worker, spouse, or parent (Van Willigen, 1997). Rather than comparing participants and nonparticipants, in this research I considered correlates of two indicators of well-being—efficacy and worry—among persons who were already volunteers. I also examined the effects of training and education activities and preferences for specific types of instruction in relation to efficacy and worry about performing tasks.

HYPOTHESES

I formulated the following hypotheses regarding voluntary activities, efficacy, and worry.

1. Training prior to becoming a volunteer, in-service training, and formal education are associated with a positive assessment of earlier training among volunteers.
2. Training prior to becoming a volunteer, in-service training, and formal education are associated with greater efficacy in performing tasks among volunteers.
3. Training prior to becoming a volunteer, in-service training, and formal education are associated with less worry about performing tasks among volunteers.
4. A positive assessment of earlier training is associated with less worry about performing tasks among volunteers.
5. Greater efficacy is associated with less worry about performing tasks among volunteers.

I formulated no hypotheses about relationships between preferences for eight specific education and training activities and well-being. Demographic characteristics (age and gender) were included in the analyses, but no hypotheses were made about them.

MEASURES

Respondents indicated if greater availability of the following eight education and training activities would assist them in their current efforts: (1) more opportunities for meetings with other volunteers, (2) written materials on advocacy in long-term care, (3) written materials on understanding the needs of older people, (4) time allocated to teaching skills and techniques advocates need to know, (5) opportunities to attend conferences and workshops on long-term care, (6) opportunities to make decisions on their own, (7) time for individual talks with their supervisor, and (8) more frequent checks of their work by the supervisor. Responses were coded "0" if additional activities were not needed and "1" if they were needed.

Assessment of the adequacy of training was measured with the following statement: "Before I became a volunteer resident advocate, it would have helped to have had more instruction about what is expected from volunteers ("Strongly agree" [1] to "Strongly disagree" [5]). A higher score indicated more adequate training. The presence or absence of training was measured by the following questions: "Did you receive formal orientation training through a workshop or some other method for your duties as an advocate?" (80 percent yes) and "Have you received additional formal training for your tasks beyond your initial orientation training?" (63 percent yes). "Yes" was coded "0" and "no" was coded "1."

Six items measured efficacy on a five-point scale ("Strongly agree" [1] to "Strongly disagree" [5]). Representative statements were "Sometimes I feel I have little control over my activities," "I believe there are positive changes I can make in the lives of residents," and "I sometimes feel helpless in deciding how best to approach the problems and complaints of residents." The six items were summed. Data were coded so that a higher score reflected greater efficacy (alpha = .67).

Worry and concern about carrying out the tasks of a volunteer advocate were measured by three items that were summed: "I worry about not being able to fulfill my responsibility as a volunteer, "There are times when I feel I do not do enough for the residents," and "As a volunteer, it is sometimes unclear what I should do for residents." Response categories were coded so that a high score indicated greater worry ("Strongly agree" [5] to "Strongly disagree" [1], alpha = .58). These items included concern about fulfilling obligations as well as a question about adequate knowledge of tasks.

RESULTS

Volunteers indicated whether eight training and education activities would help them in their current work (table 10.1). The two types of activities needed by the largest proportion of individuals vary in the ease with which they might be accommodated. The largest proportion of persons would have liked more materials on understanding the needs of older people (38 percent). This preference may be easier to address than the preference that more time be given to teaching them skills and techniques resident advocates need to know (36 percent). Almost 30 percent wanted more opportunities for group meetings with other resident advocates, and more than one-quarter (27 percent) believed they

Table 10.1
Preferred Training/Education Activities and Materials of Volunteers (N = 777)

	Percentage Who Prefer More Activities
Written materials on understanding older people	38
Time allocated to teaching skills and techniques for advocacy	36
Meetings with other volunteers	29
Written materials on advocacy in long-term care	27
Attendance at conferences and workshops on long-term care	26
Increased time with supervisor	11
Opportunities to make decisions	7
More frequent checks on work by supervisor	6

would benefit from additional written materials on advocacy in long-term care. Another quarter would have liked to attend conferences and workshops about long-term care. A minority of volunteers expressed interest in the three remaining activities: more frequent supervision of their work (6 percent), increased opportunities to make decisions on their own (7 percent), and more time for individual interaction with their supervisor (11 percent). The most frequent preferences tended to be for education, training, or materials, whereas the least-needed activities pertained to increased supervision, greater autonomy in their work as advocates, and time to interact with a supervisor.

Assessment of Earlier Training

In the multivariate analysis of the assessment of earlier training, needs for eight education and training activities, initial and follow-up training, and demographic characteristics (age, education, and gender) were studied. Inspection of a reduced model showed that six variables contributed significantly to a preference for more training (table 10.2).

The hypothesis about the relationship between formal education, training, and assessment of early training was partially supported. Persons with more formal education and who had received training prior to assuming their tasks found fewer limitations in their preparation for volunteer work. Volunteers with higher levels of formal education had also more often received both initial and in-service training ($r = .11, .13, p < .01$, respectively).

Table 10.2
Multiple Regressions of Education/Training Needs and Experiences, Demographic Characteristics, Assessment of Training, Efficacy, and Worry about Responsibilities of Volunteers (N = 754)

	Assessment of Initial Training			Efficacy			Worry		
	r	Beta	t	r	Beta	t	r	Beta	t
Gender	.09	.09	2.70**	--	--	--	--	--	--
Education	.07	.10	2.75**	.13	.09	2.26*	--	--	--
Initial training	-.13	.10	-3.05***	--	--	--	--	--	--
Assessment of initial training	--	--	--	.25	.27	6.96***	.33	.23	6.78***
Inservice training	--	--	--	-.11	-.09	-2.50**			
Education/training needs									
Meetings with other volunteers	-.20	-.10	-2.76**	--	--	--	--	--	--
Written materials on advocacy	-.21	-.16	-4.45***	--	--	--	--	--	--
Training/advocacy skills	-.20	-.20	-5.64***	--	--	--	-.14	-.09	-2.85**
Increased time with supervisor	--	--	--	-.11	-.10	-2.52**	--	--	--
Efficacy	--	--	--	--	--	--	.43	.38	11.49***
Worry	--	--	--	--	--	--	--	--	--
R^2		.13			.11			.26	

*$p < .05$
**$p < .01$
***$p < .001$
[a] Only significant values are presented.

Volunteers who believed more training was needed prior to assuming their role continued to express needs for training and educational activities. A greater allocation of time devoted to learning needed skills and access to written materials on advocacy were the two most important correlates of a preference for more and earlier training. Those who would have benefited from earlier instruction wanted more opportunities to meet as a group with other volunteers. Men were a little more likely than women to note a need for more instruction prior to becoming a volunteer resident advocate.

Efficacy

Preferences for eight training and educational activities, assessment of earlier training, prior and follow-up training, and demographic characteristics (age, gender, and education) made up the multivariate analysis of efficacy (table 10.2). Four variables were important determinants of efficacy of volunteer advocates. Partially supporting the hypothesis, both formal education and follow-up training enhanced efficacy, but initial training did not affect efficacy. Negative assessment of earlier training was the most important factor in diminishing efficacy. Of the eight needs for education and training activities, only a preference for more time to work with a supervisor was associated with less efficacy.

Worry

Preferences for eight training and educational activities, assessment of earlier training, efficacy, prior training, and demographic characteristics were included in the multivariate analysis of worry about volunteer work (table 10.2). As hypothesized, volunteers who described higher levels of efficacy and more positive assessments of early training were less worried about fulfilling their responsibilities to residents. Contrary to the hypothesis, actual initial and inservice training and formal education did not directly diminish worry. Rather, education and initial training affected efficacy, which in turn reduced worry. A preference for only one of the eight education and training activities was associated with worry about work as a volunteer; a need for more time allocated to learning skills of an ombudsmen was related to greater worry.

DISCUSSION

The literature tends to be uniformly positive about the usefulness of training. This research investigated the extent to which experiences and reflections on training and education affected the outcomes of volunteers. Support for hypotheses about relationships between assessments of training and education, efficacy, and worry was mixed.

Corresponding to other findings about formal education and efficacy (Bandura, 1997), persons with higher levels of education were more confident about their efficacy as volunteers. Through its effect on efficacy, education diminished worry. Even though formal education was attained decades earlier, its influence extended over a lifetime.

A positive evaluation of early training as a volunteer also had a long reach, reflected in its direct effect in fostering efficacy and reducing worry about meeting responsibilities in the ombudsman program. Regardless of the actual quality of the training experience, the subjective assessment was important in sustaining well-being (Baruch & Barnett, 1987).

Most expressions of need for training and education by volunteers were benign and not linked with well-being. In fact, only four of the eight preferences for training and education activities affected assessment of earlier training, efficacy, or worry. When preferences for additional training and education activities were significantly associated with well-being, however, expressing a need was related to more worry and less efficacy.

Practitioners and researchers advise others on techniques of investigation, education, and training of volunteers that they have found to be effective (Dancy & Wynn-Dancy, 1995; Duncan, 1995), and some identify best practices (Hunt, 2000). This research provided an opportunity to compare outcomes for volunteers who had or had not received training before they were to perform a complex task.

Contrary to the hypotheses, initial and follow-up training were not consistently and directly related to the assessment of training or well-being. Despite the view that training may be a form of caring for volunteers and the expectation that it will have positive effects (Scott & Caldwell, 1996), participation per se in training prior to becoming an advocate did not diminish worry or enhance efficacy. The absence of consistent, positive outcomes of training may be attributable to a number of factors. Types and quality of training activities varied across settings in which volunteers worked. It would have been useful to have had more detailed quantitative and qualitative information on their training experiences and to measure them in relation to outcomes.

Continued in-service training is recommended for established volunteers (Duncan, 1995; Hunt, 2000), and the preference of volunteers is for ongoing training. Follow-up training did increase feelings of efficacy, which in turn diminished worry of these volunteers.

Supporting other literature, there was a link between feelings of efficacy and less worry (Davey, Jubb, & Cameron, 1996). Those who believed they could solve problems that occurred in their work as advocate were less worried. Research suggests that believing one can implement solutions may be more important to well-being than generating options to address problems (Bandura, 1997).

Findings supported the thinking that efficacy is a powerful social-psychological resource for well-being (Mirowsky & Ross, 1986). From the standpoint of practice, it is important to know that in-service training heightened feelings of mastery of volunteers and in doing so, contributed to an important resource on which to draw. Although years of formal education may be altered little for most older volunteers, provision of in-service training should be more attainable. For those who work with volunteers, it is useful to realize that enhancing self-efficacy raises the motivation to perform (Eden & Kinnar, 1991).

Chapter 11

Images of Volunteerism

Personal Descriptions of Benefits, Advice, and Recommendations

---

This chapter provides insight into volunteers' views and thoughts about being an advocate after they had been participants for a while. They commented on the benefits and rewards of volunteering for themselves personally and also shared advice for those who would follow them. After having participated, volunteers indicated why they would or would not become involved in the activities again. Volunteers' attitudes toward their tasks reflected the long reach of the activities as they affected not only conceptions of their work as advocates but also their influence on views of their own lives as older persons.

In an ethnographic study, Hasselkus (1988) elicited information on the meaning of the caregiving experience. Some of the themes of meaning derived by Hasselkus are useful in thinking about the outcomes of volunteering. Although these volunteers were not direct caregivers, they were responsible for improving and ensuring quality of care. Hasselkus (1988, p. 686) observed that meaning refers to those "values, beliefs, and principles that people use to organize their behavior and to interpret their experience." Based on ethnographic interviews, she described five themes of meaning in caregiving: sense of self, sense of managing, sense of fear and risk, sense of change in role and responsibility, and sense of the future. Themes of meaning typify shared experiences of those who were involved in aspects of caring. As they relate to the influence of volunteering on individuals, these themes may entail shifts in conceptions of the self, strain from the management of roles, sometimes unanticipated responsibilities, unexpected concerns for others, and possibly, changes in perceptions of their own future.

The values and beliefs that guided individuals in their activities as volunteers became clearer as they shared their views on the most difficult aspects of being advocates (see chapter 4). In this chapter, participants relate positive features of their role, advice for others, and the influence of volunteering on their conceptions of nursing facilities. Through individuals' comments, one can see how their conceptions of themselves as volunteers ranged from the altruistic and humanistic to the strained, the instrumental, the uncertain and to the few who would reject this type of voluntarism again.

The chapter concludes with the contribution of volunteering to altered images of individuals' own futures and changed perceptions of nursing facilities. Throughout, beliefs and values that volunteers used to organize their behavior and to interpret their experiences as they assisted others and thought about their joys and troubles are revealed.

Some of the most stressful and the most satisfying aspects of volunteering emanated from direct contact with residents. Even rewarding interaction with residents, however, may involve ongoing management of emotional concerns by the volunteer. The themes derived from responses to the various questions are general and were identified for the purposes of understanding the multiplicity of satisfactions and demands experienced by advocates. There are no doubt instances of overlapping themes of benefits, advice, and recommendations. Even so, I have attempted to enumerate and provide examples of the general themes that were studied.

BENEFITS FROM VOLUNTEERING

Volunteers described some of the positive features of being a resident advocate. The responses were categorized into five groups of benefits (table 11.1).

Contact with Appreciative Residents

The positive aspect noted by the largest proportion of volunteers was visiting and having contact with appreciative residents (46 percent). A man in his eighties identified the most positive thing about being a volunteer as "Visiting with people you have known. Getting acquainted with people who appreciate you and helping them to accept the change in their living conditions." Another volunteer commented, "The love and appreciation of the residents for my just 'being there' to CARE and LISTEN is rewarding to me" (female, age 63). There is an "opportunity to talk to residents and listen to them. The residents appreciate anything that is done for them" (female, age 75).

A volunteer in her sixties identified the best aspect of participation as "Positive contact with residents by observing and listening." Another volunteer noted her objectives: "Getting to know some of those beautiful older people. Trying to bring some 'sunshine' to a lonely heart" (female, age 68). "They appreciate us so much." "The most positive aspects are seeing how much the residents enjoy the interviews, seeing how grateful they are for any problems we can solve, and meeting many nice people and families" (female, age 81).

Table 11.1
Benefits of Volunteering

Benefits	Percentage (*N*=694)
Contact with appreciative residents	46
Making a difference	29
Personal gratification and positive feelings	12
Preparation for the future	6
Interaction with facility staff	6

Volunteers elaborated on two further aspects of their relationships with residents that resulted from their positive contacts with them. Opportunities for reciprocity to occur and to form friendships with residents were important benefits to volunteers that ensued from their interaction with them.

Reciprocity

Volunteers described several elements of reciprocity in their relationships with residents. "I feel I gain more from visiting and listening to residents than I give them" (female, age 64). "I receive much more than I can ever give" (female, 81 years). Another facet of exchange extended beyond interaction with individual residents: "I can give back some time and effort to the facility as my mother was in another facility before her death, and I wish I had known more about the ombudsman program" (female, age 82). The satisfaction of giving something back is a salient reward of volunteering (Scheibel, 1996; Wilson, 2000).

Friendship

Opportunities for friendships and contact with residents believed to have limited social ties were among the benefits noted. "The friendships you make with residents are very rewarding. Some people don't get visitors so they are very appreciative of whatever you do for them" (female, age 63). A woman in her eighties observed, "The heartfelt thanks and joy my visits seem to bring to the residents is overpowering. All residents seem to need visitors (besides their relatives) and they are so thankful." "Residents need friends."

Making a Difference

Some volunteers described making a difference in residents' lives as the most positive aspect of their work (29 percent). "If you can help one person, the time spent is worthwhile" (male, age 75). A woman in her seventies observed that the best part is "trying to improve the lives of the residents and the good feeling that you are making a difference." "Trying to provide a quality of life for residents and still make them feel useful" is a positive aspect (female, 55 years). "Helping the families iron out problems with their loved ones in the nursing facility makes a difference" (female, age 74).

A woman in her sixties clearly articulated how she believed she brought about change. "If I can improve the service in my residents' life, such as CALL LIGHTS, food preparation, etc. and bring them joy, and the knowledge that someone cares and intends to help whenever possible, I feel I have accomplished something very worthwhile." "Being able to bring quality living to a nursing home" is a benefit. "I'm able to share what I believe are good working techniques with the elderly" (female, age 53). "I feel I can spend time with residents. The work I see done is very important and done with great care. We give assurance to the public as well as to residents that they are getting quality care" (female, age not given). Making a difference in the lives of others was a benefit of volunteering and a reason for continued participation.

Personal Gratification and Positive Feelings

Twelve percent of respondents specifically described the greatest benefits from volunteering as the personal gratification and positive feelings they experienced. These responses to volunteering focused on feelings of volunteers. This benefit, of course, probably overlaps with those attributed to visiting, contact with appreciative residents, and making a difference. A woman in her seventies commented, "It just feels good!" Respondents expressed the benefits in other ways: "The feeling you get when you visit and see the smiles on their faces. Knowing that you are there if they should need someone" (female, age 68). "The warm reaction by most of the residents and the good feeling I experience when interviewing the residents" are benefits (female, age 73). A woman age 54 articulated her specific personal gratification: "As I enter the facility, I feel a sense of peace—a slowing from the frantic pace of life outside—a calmness. Most of the time the residents are very happy to visit with me. I almost always feel lifted in spirit after my visits with the residents."

Volunteers' Thoughts of Their Present and Future

In addition to their other views, some volunteers specifically remarked about the benefits of volunteering for clarifying their own futures or their present relative advantages (6 percent). A man in his seventies observed, "It makes me personally realize that I may someday be in same situation as the residents I now visit." A man, age 80, noted that he now had "strong feeling of empathy toward totally helpless residents—there except for the grace of God go I." A woman, age 69, added: "Sympathy with residents' feelings is developed. Understanding their needs helps me foresee my future needs." "Being in touch with the residents should make volunteers appreciate their own abilities and freedoms" (female, age 82). Finally, a woman (age 77) observed that "preparing oneself to be a resident" was a benefit of volunteering. Volunteers in this group often reflected on their own advantages tempered with thoughts about their possible future needs.

Interaction with the Staff

The opportunity to meet staff, to discuss complaints with them, and to see the good job they did were positive aspects for 6 percent of the volunteers. Being able to report complaints from residents to staff members was a benefit, although some questioned its effectiveness. A female volunteer observed: "We, at least, report the residents' complaints; whether they're carried out or not is questionable. I don't feel we have any clout." "Residents have someone they can complain to about their care. They say it doesn't do any good to complain though" (female, age 74). "If volunteers had more respect by management and were listened to and some of the suggestions followed or completed, it would be more positive" (female, age 68).

Others viewed the staff more positively and understood constraints under which they worked. "Appreciating the high quality of care that is given to residents by the facility staff" was a positive aspect for one volunteer. A benefit was "a feeling of being useful. Seeing how a long-term facility operates. I have gotten a real appreciation of the valuable work CNA's do everyday" (female, age 70). "There are no pressures from staff members. There are wonderful accommodations. The facility is very friendly to my visits" (male, age 77). "Residents also have someone to help with things that they cannot ask a staff member" (female, 83). A woman age 40 remarked, "I am in a great facility—lots of caring is happening." These positive views contrasted with those who questioned whether their efforts were taken seriously and acted upon.

REASONS FOR CONTINUED PARTICIPATION

One indicator of job satisfaction may be whether an individual would enter the same occupation, take the same or similar position again, or recommend it to others. Decisions about continuing volunteer work may involve some of the same processes. Reasons individuals gave for continued participation or nonparticipation as volunteers were thought to be reflections of their satisfaction.

Respondents indicated whether they would become a volunteer advocate if they were able to begin again. The majority (82 percent) would participate again. Others also have observed high satisfaction among advocates (Nelson, 1995). In response to an unstructured question, volunteers gave reasons they would choose to be involved as an advocate again. These reasons formed four general themes: satisfying activities (30 percent), making a difference (27 percent), enjoying being with people (23 percent), meeting specific needs of the aged (16 percent), and other (4 percent). The reasons for continuation in large part parallel the benefits observed by volunteers and are not discussed separately.

Reasons for Nonparticipation

Five percent ($n = 39$) would not participate if they were starting again. The views of this smaller number of those who would choose not to be involved or were unsure should be taken into account. Primary decisions for nonparticipation may be categorized into program barriers and personal difficulties; other reasons were less frequently noted.

Program Barriers

Program barriers as reasons to withdraw (35 percent) included frustrations in carrying out the complaint process, which resulted in questions about the effectiveness of volunteers. Program barriers included the following: "The program does not work," a "lack of communication within the program." A 53-year-old woman commented, "I don't enjoy conflict." A younger man noted, "It is frustrating to listen to volunteers record the same complaints over and over." A 58-year-old woman alluded to difficulties she encountered in reporting complaints: "It is not very rewarding except for those who only visit and pat staff people on the back. They are more welcome than those who point out concerns." A woman (age 61) noted, "Time spent was ignored or ineffective." Finally a man (age 70) asked, "Are we appreciated?" For this group of volunteers who would not participate again, more training might have aided them in managing complaints.

Personal Difficulties

Two general types of personal difficulties contributed to ambiguity about future participation: (1) role conflicts and burdens attributed to the amount of time needed (30 percent) and (2) feeling inadequate for various reasons ("too old," poor health, 22 percent). For some, these factors were combined; for example, an 83-year-old female volunteer explained why she was unsure about serving again: "It's not because I do not like it, but health and lack of time interfere. Also, I have many family activities and trips."

For others, uncertainty related to the magnitude of responsibility entailed in volunteers' tasks: "It's a big responsibility." A woman in her eighties wondered "if I am doing all I can for the residents." Another commented, "Not being able to do more for the residents is a problem" (female, age 71). Still others noted that they needed more volunteers and help on their committees. The concerns of volunteers about carrying out their responsibilities may in part be addressed by continued mentoring and training.

As discussed further below, worry about fulfilling responsibilities also figured in the views of those who were uncertain about their future participation. In answer to a structured question, 45 percent of all volunteers, not just limited to those who would not participate again, acknowledged that they worried about not fulfilling their responsibilities as advocates.

Reasons for Uncertainty about Participation

Role Conflict and Time Constraints

A larger group ($n = 104$), about 13 percent of the sample, felt unsure about whether they would participate if they were starting anew. In contrast to reasons given by those who would not become an advocate again, those with ambiguous feelings about participating again tended to give only personal reasons and focused little on hindrances attributable to the program. Once again, conflict with work and family roles and burdens of time commitments were among the dominant personal reasons (41 percent). Time constraints were not barriers solely for the younger employed volunteers. A woman over age 90 observed, "I can't give it enough time."

Feelings of Inadequacy and Responsibility

The other major reasons for uncertainty about continuing were more directly related to competency and to performance of volunteer tasks. These were feelings of inadequacy (28 percent) and too much responsibility (13 percent). For some, uncertainty about participation was increased by the nature of the tasks. "I have to push myself to make visits. Most residents are unable to communicate. Families are sometimes present which helps" (female, age 64). "I feel like I have too much responsibility" (female, age 59). Both feelings of inadequacy and too much responsibility may be more easily addressed to increase retention than resolution of role overload and time constraints involving work and family.

Volunteers' reasons for not participating again and reasons for uncertainty about future involvement were similar, with a major exception. Those who would not participate again, compared with those who were uncertain, cited program barriers, including difficulties with the complaint process, much more frequently as a reason they would not be involved. Burdens from much responsibility, however, affected all volunteers—those who would not participate again, those who were uncertain, and those who planned to continue.

REASONS FOR RESIGNATION OF ADVOCATES

Time Constraints and Health

Volunteers identified major reasons that fellow advocates left their work. The most frequently noted reasons were a lack of time or being busy (30 percent) and health problems (23 percent; table 11.2). Descriptions of these reasons were usually straightforward, such as "poor health" or "too busy." Demands from both paid work and other volunteer activities were among the factors noted.

For example, some have "conflict with other volunteer responsibilities" (female, age 73). "Some have other jobs that interfere. Some just get tired of it" (male, age 77). "Some who leave lack commitment and put other things as more important" (female, age 77). "We've only lost one volunteer due to death. Reasons are 'lack of time and patience' " (female, age 75). Regardless of whether the volunteers would participate again, time constraints were a most consistent threat to their continued involvement. Schiman and Lordeman (1989) found illness or change in health and other commitments to be two of the other most common reasons volunteers resign. Burnout was a third reason for resignation of volunteers.

Burnout

Some respondents mentioned aspects of burnout (15 percent) as a reason for resignations of volunteers (table 11.2). Frustration from barriers to resolution of complaints and depression resulting from conditions of residents fostered burnout of these volunteers.

Frustration and the Lack of Change

Perhaps not surprisingly, reasons for leaving were similar to some of the greatest difficulties identified by volunteers. Some persons were more explicit about possible reasons for burnout and questioned their effectiveness and their efficacy in the complaint process.

A man, age 75, wrote about resignation of volunteers, "I think they get tired and feel burned out." "They burn out" (female, age 73). "Some say they need to get away from it for awhile" (male, age 73). "They burn out and have the feeling they aren't making a difference" (female, 71 years). "Do we really make a difference?" (female, age 54). Volunteers are "tired of lack of change by administrators, staff" (male, 33 years). "You can't always see results. With turnover of administration, staff and residents it's difficult to develop a working relationship" (female, 64 years). There is the "frustration of the more things change the more they stay the same" (female, 77 years). People leave because "no action is taken on residents' complaints" (female, age not given) and

Table 11.2
Reasons Volunteers Resign

Reasons	Percentage (N=645)
Time constraints	30
Health problems	23
Burnout	15
Age	12
Migration	7
Lack of training	6
Other	6

"feeling the management ignores your criticism (female, age 61). "In our situation the administrator of the nursing home wouldn't cooperate with us. She didn't like being told when things weren't going right" (female, age 65). "They [volunteers] lack appreciation for their efforts and are often viewed suspiciously by facility staff (female, age 58). This group of respondents attributed withdrawal from volunteering primarily to frustration with the quality of reception their activities received by personnel in nursing facilities.

Depression

For other volunteers, reasons for burnout involved their personal response to visits with residents. Depression and discouragement were among the greatest hardships noted by advocates, and they were implicated in resignation from volunteering, for example, "Most likely the patients and their health problems can be depressing for volunteers especially their mental problems and memory etc." (female, age 67). "Frustration and depression at visiting such a depressing place" are reasons for leaving (female, age 72). "They are not able to handle the changes which come about in people they once knew out in the community who are not as independent or able to care for themselves" (female, age 45). "It's depressing; there is burnout—not enough folks for all the visits—scary. It's not for them" (female, age 55). Among these persons, resignation of volunteers was attributed to their personal reaction to changes in residents and visiting. The behavior ascribed to volunteers who resigned was in response to illness, disability, or deterioration of residents with whom they may have had contact rather than problems with more instrumental aspects of the complaint process.

Age and Migration

Twelve percent of the respondents mentioned age as the reason that volunteers leave their work in the ombudsman program. A woman noted, "Myself now I will soon be 81. I need to slow down. I do other volunteer work also." A man (age 71) observed: "Most volunteers are retirees, and many go to warmer climates in the winter and thereby do not serve the full year. They then get out of the notion to serve." Seven percent noted moving away from the area as a reason for resigning from volunteer work. The good health and higher educational levels of advocates are likely also factors that contribute to migration.

Lack of Training

Although some of the other reasons volunteers resign may be indirectly due to training, some advocates (6 percent) specifically observed that a lack of training was a major reason for turnover. The implication of their comments was that through training, volunteers not only will have an accurate perception of their duties, but they will also obtain skills that enable them to handle both routine and more troublesome tasks. For example, a woman in her sixties observed, "They don't know what the duties are before they say they'll do it." "There is not enough preparation. They become overwhelmed."

These findings contrasted with views of nearly half of another sample of volunteers who concluded that "adequate training" is one of the most important factors affecting retention (Schiman & Lordeman, 1989). For the older advocates studied here, however, reasons other than unsatisfactory training were more salient in the decision to withdraw from voluntarism. Generally, however, perceptions of factors leading to resignation from volunteering paralleled those found by others. Schiman and Lordeman also identified illness, aspects of burnout, stress, commitments, and schedule conflicts as reasons for termination of volunteer services. Reasons for termination often mirrored the greatest hardships identified by advocates. Burnout may be tempered somewhat by better training, but major reasons for termination such as changes in health, migration, or time commitments are less amenable to intervention.

RECOMMENDATIONS FOR TRAINING

Volunteers gave recommendations for training persons who might become advocates in the future. A majority of the suggestions were not specific and called for training in general.

Prior and Continued Training

The most frequently offered admonition was to obtain training before assuming duties as volunteer (34 percent). A related recommendation was to continue training yearly and attend meetings (17 percent). A corollary was to review the manual for volunteers frequently (9 percent). The suggestion for prior training may seem as though it should be unnecessary to mention, but 20 percent indicated they had received no training. A woman in her sixties described what it was like not to have training: "I was a volunteer for six months—so I wasn't sure what I was doing for that long until we had the district meeting."

Additional volunteers called for training at particular times. "Some type of training should be given to all new members—perhaps by the local area agency on aging" (male, age 70). One recommended, "Have good training and every three months all should get together to review the work" (male, age 66). Another suggested, "Go to all the meetings you can go to. You never learn enough" (female, age 62). "Our yearly group training has been good" (female, age 54). "Allow time for more questions by volunteers" (female, age 61).

Other volunteers' thoughts on the nature of training were more specific to securing and reporting concerns of residents: "We need more relevant training on what to look for and how to interpret what we see" (male, age 60). "We need more training on communicating with residents suffering some form of dementia" (female, age 63). Some volunteers addressed the environment in which complaints are received and training for managing complaints on-site. A woman in her sixties commented, "Be thorough in training, but it would mean more if management of the facility were more receptive and corrected problems." "Make them [volunteers] understand that it is all right to bring complaints to the administrators" (female, age 76).

Others had suggestions about who should be trainers and where training should take place. "The trainers should be people who have been volunteers, who have hands-on experience. They understand the problems of volunteers best" (female, age 69). "It would be beneficial if training were done in the facility where we work" (female, age 69). "We do not need certain speakers on certain subjects. For example, a detailed presentation by a dietitian was of no help to me at all" (female, age 71).

The "Buddy" System

In response to the unstructured question about training, 18 percent recommended a "buddy" system in which a new volunteer accompanies a more-experienced one. A volunteer described a current experience: "I have recently helped a new volunteer by taking her with me to visit residents and observe the facility and staff practices. We went together on three different occasions" (female, age 63). A woman in her forties counseled, "As well as an orientation session, if possible, have a current volunteer go through a resident review with them." Other representative recommendations included the following: "I would suggest at least a workshop and then maybe accompany a volunteer on a visit before making their own initial visit" (female, age 68). "Have them observe some of our meetings and go on visits with volunteers" (male, age 77). Recommendation of the "buddy" system was the single most frequently suggested specific aspect of training. Generally, the recommendations for training were modest.

Knowledge of Aging

As a part of training, 9 percent highlighted the importance of knowing about and understanding the needs of the aged and how such knowledge would be reflected in the actions of volunteers. In response to a structured question, 38 percent of the volunteers felt that further instruction about aging and the aged would improve their performance of required activities (see chapter 10). The significance of imparting knowledge about aging was noted in several ways. "It is important to teach about older persons and their needs" (male, age 70). A woman of 69 advised, "Be faithful, caring, kind, entrusted, considerate and informed." "The residents' needs have to come first. You can't allow personal feelings to interfere. Also, they [residents] need to be trained in the program" (female, 65 years).

Another advised to instruct volunteers "to treat the resident as they would like to be treated if their roles were reversed" (female, age 82). A man in his eighties suggested, "Visit with people. ... Learn how to help them to accept the change in their living conditions."

ADVICE FOR VOLUNTEER ADVOCATES

In addition to their recommendations for training, volunteers answered the following question: "If you could give advice to others who are or may become volunteers, what would your advice be? Responses were grouped into four general themes: the importance of positive attitudes toward older persons, a view of volunteering as challenging work with personal satisfaction, recommended behavior for advocates, and regard for the time needed for advocacy.

Attitudes toward Older Persons and the Work of Advocates

Positive Attitudes toward Elders

The recommendations offered by the largest proportion of volunteers included the importance of having a positive attitude toward the elderly (28 percent; table 11.3). Feelings about older persons and dedication to others' welfare were emphasized.

Table 11.3
Advice for Future Resident Advocates

Advice	Percentage (N=660)
Positive attitudes toward older persons	28
Challenging work and personal satisfaction	27
Appropriate behavior for advocates	20
Time and advocacy	19
Other	6

As one respondent put it, "If you don't love older people nor have patience with them, don't become a volunteer. They need lots of TLC" (female, age 75). Dedication to the task was also important. "Don't [volunteer] unless you really care about the welfare of others" (female, age 68). A man in his seventies observed, "They [volunteers] must realize how important being a volunteer advocate is. They have to be very dedicated."

Friendship with Residents

In their counsel for persons who might become advocates, some volunteers emphasized primarily acting in a friendly manner with residents, cultivating sociability, and caring. A 77-year-old man suggested, "Go in with the attitude that you can do good for the resident if only as a new and loving friend. They often only need someone to talk to." "Be willing to spend time with the residents. Get to know and understand their problems. Be willing to touch or pat their backs. Be friendly" (female, age 83). "Just be a friend to the resident." One admonished, "Keep it simple—not a lot of paperwork. Let them go in as 'friendly visitors' " (female, age 80). "Establish comfortable open communication with staff supervisors" (female, age 75). "Use your heart as well as your eyes and ears and nose. Staff and residents are much more accepting if you really care" (female, age 45).

Still others suggested that volunteers could practice orientations other than that of the friendly visitor. These respondents differentiated between roles with a primary focus on advocacy or mediation and those emphasizing sociability. For example, a woman in her fifties warned, "If you only like to visit residents and tell staff members they're doing a great job, then visit without becoming a resident advocate. Volunteer membership requires being willing to speak out when residents need an advocate or when conditions are substandard." Another suggested a need for combining expressive and instrumental approaches: "One of the most impor-

tant prerequisites to becoming a volunteer ombudsman is loving and caring for
the elderly and infirm. Attitude and patience in serving as a 'middleman' between
the residents and the administration are important" (female, age 63).

Challenging Work and Personal Satisfaction

In their advice to others, volunteers also often commented about the challenging and satisfying nature of the work (27 percent). They gave reassurance
and offered encouragement to potential participants. Some described how to
focus on the residents and at the same time obtain personal benefits and satisfaction. "Don't look on it as a job but as a joyful experience" (female, 71 years).
"It's a great morale booster. Gives you the opportunity to do something good
for someone else. Do it if you believe in helping others. It makes you feel good
about yourself" (female, age 53). "It is not a burden and you always feel rewarded and thankful it is not you or a loved one there. I always feel good when
I have made my visits" (female, age 82). "It's a good educational experience.
You have a satisfaction knowing that you are doing something for yourself and
others" (male, age 77). "It makes you grateful that you have reasonably good
health. It is also gratifying to know you speak out for some of the residents that
don't speak for themselves" (female, age 67).

Another respondent echoed the importance of the tasks dedicated to the welfare of residents: "It is a very worthwhile work. Our residents need us as
sounding boards and they like the attention of someone visiting and talking to
them" (female, 83 years). Researchers stress the importance of meaningful and
challenging work for volunteers (Caro & Bass, 1995). Some of these volunteers
were fortunate enough to receive challenges and satisfaction and recommended
how others might attain these benefits.

"Appropriate" Behavior for Advocates

The advice of about 20 percent focused on behavior and approaches to their
work as a volunteer. There were numerous admonitions about volunteer conduct. A woman in her sixties, for example, advised, "Be yourself. Talk to residents like you would like to be talked to. Use simple language and be a good
listener!" Other advice described specific volunteer behavior in facilities, the
importance of a clear understanding of duties, and attentiveness to the condition of residents.

Behavior in the Facility

There was an emphasis on maintaining a presence at the facility. "Get to
know the residents personally. Keep your eyes open!! Do not be afraid to ask
the supervisors if you see and/or find something questionable. Eat at the facility once in a while and see how the residents are treated, especially the ones

who have to be fed" (female, age 81). "Go to your nursing home different times of the day and night, talk to the residents, see if they're clean, properly fed, and treated with kindness" (female, age 65). "Try to stop by the nursing home and just observe the goings on through the day. Observe their care and learn how things are done." A man in his thirties gave additional advice about what to do. "Look, listen and smell as you go through facilities. You can learn a lot by how it looks, what's being said by both residents and staff, and whether or not there are consistently strong odors." In the same vein, a woman in her sixties commented, "Learn to observe the basis of care, smell, dress quality and then enjoy visiting while noting body language and nonverbal cues." "Be observing. Listen, don't comment. Be helpful but not in the way. Learn to know the administrator and the staff members as well as possible" (male, age 70). These suggestions stressed the importance of familiarity with the facility and its staff as well as behavior with residents.

Clarifying Volunteers' Duties

Several described the importance of clarifying the activities expected of volunteers. Participants emphasized the need for clarity in duties prior to beginning work as a volunteer. A volunteer in her sixties articulated this advice: "I would like them [future volunteers] to realize what the duties are. We have some volunteers who either want to belong to everything or someone has talked them into joining telling them that they just go visit people at the nursing home." A man (age 73) suggested that potential volunteers "take a tour of a facility and visit with two or three residents to acquaint themselves with what is expected of a committee member. Take training." "Read any material the state provides for resident advocates" (female, age 70). One volunteer called attention to the views of peers who work in the same facility and asked directly, "Do you understand what the older volunteers expect of you?" (female, age 77).

Condition of Residents

Volunteers noted the need to learn about the condition of residents, to know what to expect and how it might interact with their accomplishments. New advocates should be prepared for changes in residents: "Don't be afraid of these people even though they act differently than they once did. The residents still like love and attention, a friendly smile, and a kind word" (female, age 70). "Some of the persons whom you visit are rather helpless. I think you need to know that before you start" (male, age 65). One admonished: "Be sincere and yourself when you visit the residents. Also be ready to handle any situation as the elderly are unpredictable and sometimes act like they don't want anything to do with you" (female, age 50). Another warned, "Expect anything to happen. Some patients are in a mental condition that when they see somebody walking they think it's an employee and want you to help them *right now!* Also, expect some minor depression, because most things you really can't do anything about. Many of the patients are just existing, not 'living' because of diminished physical and mental capacities" (male, age 61). An appreciation of the need for greater understanding of residents' conditions by volunteers was perhaps also reflected by 38 percent of the respondents who in answer to a structured question said they wanted more information and materials about older persons and aging.

Time and Advocacy

Volunteers gave advice about the need to be aware of the amount of time that is required (14 percent) and specifically advocated persistence in pursuing complaints (5 percent). These volunteers stressed the necessity of realizing the length of time needed for reporting complaints and following them to their conclusion.

Care and Patience in Judgment

Volunteers suggested caution in reaching conclusions about complaints and recommended that new advocates give themselves time to adjust to the work. "Don't be too quick to judge until you've heard both sides. Also be a good listener to residents. Discuss matters that can be corrected with the administrator" (female, age 76). Another commented, "Listen carefully to any complaints. Some people are confused and don't react to complaints. Do a little further investigation before jumping to conclusions. At the same time, don't ignore the complaint" (female, age 61). Another suggested, "Learn to listen well and be positive about evaluating what you hear and what you see" (female, age 69).

Advocacy Response Time

Not only were potential volunteers advised to allow themselves time to adjust personally to the work, but they were also informed about the sometimes lengthy process needed to effect some changes. Potential advocates were advised that to investigate, report, and resolve some complaints requires more than a fleeting commitment. The following comments are representative of the type of advice in this area. "Stay with the program for a good length of time. Do not make hasty judgments" (male, age 71). "Give it a long trial at least—don't give up! Be willing to spend both money and time. You will feel amply rewarded" (female, age 77). Another cautioned, "Realize you can't change 'city hall' in one day (or month). Changes take time and diplomacy" (male, age 70). A woman in her sixties commented, "Enjoy what you are doing and don't jump to conclusions." "Remember it's a slow process. Changes don't happen overnight. You can put as much time as you want into it!" (female, age 64).

"You cannot change all things, but you can make a difference" (male, age 74). In essence, resolution of complaints requires care, time, and patience.

Reassurance and Guidance

A woman in her fifties gave instructions and offered reassurance, "In your mind, place yourself in the resident's shoes. One needs good listening skills and patience and the courage to speak up for the resident. Don't become a volunteer unless you have a genuine respect for the dignity of the elderly. And, try not to feel too overwhelmed by the enormity of the responsibility. The other volunteers and the staff can give you guidance and tips" (female, age 54). Another was a bit more cautious and specific about learning how to do the work and training, "I would like to see a seasoned resident advocate make the first few visits with a new person to help them get their feet wet. It is *scary* on the first visits" (female, age 55).

Finally, others' advice was brief and generally encouraging. "Try it!" (female, 79 years); "Do it!" (female, 75 years); "Volunteer!" (female, 47 years). "Do it! It's a neat learning experience" (female, age 61). But some noted that this type of volunteering is not for everyone. One advised, "Love what you are doing, if not, get out!" (male, age 71).

THE INFLUENCE OF VOLUNTEERING ON VIEWS OF NURSING FACILITIES

Finally, I consider the lasting effect that volunteer activities may have had on participants' perceptions of nursing facilities. I expected that the volunteering experience would be graphic enough that some persons would undergo a change in their views. The volunteers had significant personal contact with nursing facilities prior to becoming advocates. The majority (84 percent), for example, had a close relative living in a nursing facility previously. At the time of the study, more than one-quarter (27 percent) currently had a close relative living in a facility.

Beyond their prior contact with care facilities through relatives or friends who were residents, volunteers indicated whether their work as advocates had changed their view of nursing facilities. Volunteering changed the perceptions of nursing facilities for 63 percent of the respondents. Volunteers described three primary kinds of changes in their views of long-term care facilities: increased appreciation of services provided by care facilities, a greater understanding of aging and needs of the aged, and negative perceptions of nursing facilities and staffing. The first type of change included mention of increased appreciation of facilities and their staff. Volunteers gained a clearer idea of the work of aides and other staff and valued their activities and performance in the face of constraints. Persons who experienced the second type of change had come to understand older persons and their needs more fully. Through interaction with residents, volunteers had a better grasp of what to expect for themselves and others. Thus, volunteers experienced both positive and negative changes in their conceptions of nursing facilities.

Increased Appreciation of Nursing Facilities

The most frequent change was an appreciation for the caring services provided to residents by the facilities (43 percent). "They are not just a place to stay out of—as many think!" (female, age 77). "I have more appreciation of the caring services they provide" (female, age 82). "I've always believed in long term care facilities. I want them to stay or be the best they can be" (female, age 53). "I am delighted to see the improvements that have been made since my mother was a nursing home resident in the 1970s" (female, age 69). "Many of the caregivers are so great to the residents" (female, age 53). A woman remarked, "I used to think it was very depressing—but with our help—people are well taken care of." It has "made me more aware of the need for good care facilities" (male, age 73). For these volunteers, perceptions of the nature of facilities changed in a positive way.

An increased appreciation of nursing facilities that came from observing the quality of care abated the fears of some volunteers. As one respondent noted, "I'm not so frightened of perhaps having to face the prospect of becoming a resident myself. I see good care being given" (female, age 70). Another volunteer declared that "I would not be against becoming a resident in one" (female, age 69). Yet another stated that she now realized that "there is a need and purpose for them [nursing facilities]" (female, age 73). A reduction in fear of becoming a resident was a prominent transition.

The allayed fears of some were accompanied by a determination to continue to make changes. "I no longer have a fear of being in one; however, I want to make all the changes I can make to make them a better place to be" (male, age 54). Although volunteers' views of life in facilities had changed, their interest in improving conditions was unabated. For some, a new appreciation of nursing facilities focused on the specific positive contributions of staff. For example, one noted, "I have a greater appreciation of the work required by the nurses to keep their patients comfortable and mentally challenged" (female, age 68).

Understanding of Aging and Needs of the Aged

As a part of their altered views of facilities, some volunteers noted that they had obtained a greater understanding of the aging process and that their expectations of behaviors and attitudes of older persons had been clarified. As a part of this change, they realized the importance of activities of volunteers in ombudsman programs. Thus, for some volunteers, the change in perceptions of nursing facilities was in the increased importance they assigned to their work as advocates. "We are needed. The facilities need to be kept on their toes" (female, age 70). "I've seen a difference in the way some staff people treat residents if they know they are being observed from when they are unaware of it" (female, age 58). "I hope they continue to have this program when my turn comes for a nursing home" (female, age 62). "It has helped me realize more of the problems we have and how the laws have changed and we must also" (female, age 75). In documenting the change in their opinions of nursing facilities, these respondents described their recognition of the need for and the salience of their work as advocates in improving the care of residents.

Negative Thoughts about Nursing Facilities

The most negative changes in volunteers' views of facilities concerned perceptions of staff. Volunteers cautioned, "Some (facilities) try to get by on the very least (staff, etc.). They need reminders that these residents are #1 important" (female, age 45). "A good looking facility isn't necessarily a good facility. They are better than they used to be regarding activities and getting residents out of the facility" (female, age 52). "Realize even in midst of good there can be abuse" (male, age 60). "A lot of the aides have no-care attitudes, are lazy, and do not have enough experience" (female, age 65). "I feel we cannot get good aides; some want a paycheck with no care for people that really need to be loved" (female, age 80). "Care is inconsistent because help is difficult to get and keep. I know long-term staff people who are kept on because it would be hard to replace them even when they are obviously in the wrong occupation" (female, age 58). "I realize there are many problems I didn't know about—one, being able to hire caring employees" (female, age 71).

A man in his seventies simply summarized the change in his view, a perspective noted in many committee minutes and reports: "The facilities need more help." "There is too big of a work load on each aide, and the resident gets neglected" (female, age 74). One respondent concluded, "I've learned something about what makes a good one [facility]" (female, age 66).

Finally, 4 percent of the persons in this group concluded they would not want to live in a facility. "I think they are undesirable places" (female, age not given). "I hope I never have to be in one" (female, age 65). "Beware" (female, age 61). For most, however, volunteering resulted in compassion for staff and their hardships. The shortages of staff that were often the focus of resident complaints were seen by some volunteers as stressors for staff who remained.

This chapter has shown the complexity of the tasks of volunteers in an ombudsman program. In addition to knowledge about aging and investigative procedures, the practice of advocacy requires developing and maintaining relationships with residents, their families, staff, administrators, supervisors of volunteers, and peer volunteers.

Most volunteers interacted regularly with residents who had a wide range of physical and mental capacities and an array of other personal circumstances that may inspire, evoke compassion, or anger. The personal circumstances of residents may combine with positive and negative staff practices to shape the future attitudes of volunteers toward care facilities. For the majority of participants, however, the experience of volunteering changed their views of nursing facilities and in a positive way.

Chapter 12

Concluding Thoughts about
Implications for Practice

As noted in earlier chapters, available publications and manuals set forth the best practices for long-term care ombudsman programs, including the recommended content of volunteer training (Hunt, 2000). In contrast, the observations in the present book are primarily those of volunteers. Based on accounts of volunteers, this book details their reflections on practices of which they were a part, personal outcomes of their experiences, and their admonitions for others.

One intent of this chapter is to show how findings from somewhat dissimilar sources of data may have common threads that support comparable implications for practice. Observations from the early expectations of applicants, their later, actual experiences as volunteers recounted in their own words, their responses to structured questions, and outcomes of their work on committees are integrated to direct attention to needs of volunteers. Many of the suggested applications, however, are not unique to volunteers in ombudsman programs. I have made an effort here to demonstrate points at which findings from the various types of data corroborate one another to the extent that some recommendations for practice may be offered.

THE CONTEXT OF ADVOCATES' WORK

What features of the circumstances of their work described by participants inform recommendations for ombudsman or other programs with volunteers? How were somewhat conflicting perceptions of aspects of their work reconciled, and what are their implications for practice?

First, what positive aspects of their work did volunteers highlight? In response to structured questions, for example, volunteers related that their work as advocates was very important to them (90 percent) and that it had positive effects on other aspects of their lives as well (87 percent). They reported that they worked with volunteer colleagues who were highly committed to resident advocate activities (89 percent) and that their good personal relationships with these fellow volunteers were one reason they continued in the program (72 percent). Most volunteers believed that their complaints were handled effectively (73 percent), that residents were usually interested in talking with them (76 percent), and that the majority had a committee coordinator (supervisor) with whom they could openly discuss their problems (81 percent). These features of their work indicated that volunteers had a reservoir of goodwill from which to address remaining aspects of their activities that troubled them.

Against a backdrop of rewarding activities as advocates, however, some volunteers worried about not fulfilling their responsibilities as committee members (45 percent), sometimes found their activities depressing (41 percent), were sometimes unclear about what was expected of them in helping residents (38 percent), and at times found it very difficult to observe how residents were treated (35 percent). Even in the midst of quite positive involvement, almost one-third had contemplated withdrawing from their volunteer activity. This response highlights the fragility of retention and the importance of caring for volunteers even in the presence of relatively high satisfaction and positive circumstances enjoyed by the majority.

CARING FOR VOLUNTEERS

Hindrances and Difficulties

Hindrances identified by volunteers reflected barriers to their effectiveness as advocates. Identification of some hindrances suggests areas in which volunteers need to acquire skills or have better direction. Although the hindrances noted may not have specifically mentioned training, it was often directly or indirectly implicated in the needs that were expressed.

Condition of Residents

In response to a list of potential hindrances, volunteers most frequently named the frail condition of residents as a source of hindrance (see chapter 5). Volunteers also felt constrained in their work to some extent by residents' conditions (see chapter 4 for volunteers' description of this). Some volunteers reflected this hindrance by expressing a need for techniques for communicating with highly impaired residents. Managing interaction with the most ill residents was anticipated as a difficulty by volunteers when they were applicants, and it remained a concern when they were more experienced (see chapter 4). Both experienced and inexperienced volunteers identified training in communication with residents as a need. Concern for improved communication with frail clients by volunteers is not unique to participants in ombudsman programs.

Inadequate Volunteer Training

The second most frequently mentioned hindrance was inadequately trained peer volunteers. Not only were poorly trained peers identified as an important barrier; they also figured prominently in accounting for several social-psychological outcomes of participation for other volunteers. Viewing inadequately trained volunteers as a hindrance was consistently linked with negative outcomes for volunteers. Hindrances from poor training diminished effectiveness in handling complaints, increased role strain, decreased general effectiveness, and were associated with perceived needs for greater support (see chapter 5). Consequently, the efforts of well-prepared advocates were sometimes undermined by their less-skilled peers.

Clarifying the Role of Volunteers

In response to an unstructured question concerning recommendations for training, a number of respondents to the questionnaire noted the need for greater clarity in the duties of advocates (see chapter 11). Clarifying duties and the means to carry them out is especially critical for newer, less-experienced volunteers. Improved training should, of course, bring greater clarity. Even so, clearly stated responsibilities and expectations of resident advocates need to be provided to potential volunteers early in the application process.

Volunteers requested a description of the organizational hierarchy that may be involved in the complaint and investigative process. Advocates asked that the relationship between the volunteers and residents, facility personnel, the volunteer coordinator, the Area Agency on Aging, the Department of Elder Affairs, and the state Department of Inspection and Appeals, which conducts periodic surveys of nursing facilities, be articulated more clearly in their training. Some volunteers requested not only that functions of volunteers be clarified but that their activities be given greater visibility in facilities and to residents' families.

Incongruence between Anticipated and Actual Difficulties

Data from the application form and the questionnaire provided a longitudinal perspective on expectations prior to becoming a volunteer and reflections on later experiences. Incongruence between expected problems and those actually experienced may point to concerns that should be addressed. Some of the differences in perceptions of applicants and what they then observed as volunteers were marked.

Almost 40 percent of the applicants foresaw no difficulties. In contrast, with experience, most volunteers described difficult aspects of their work. Time constraints were a prominent difficulty noted by practicing volunteers (37 percent), but only 5 percent of the applicants had anticipated such demands. Time requirements were also reasons for volunteers resigning. An accurate indication of the amount of time needed for their activities should be provided to prospective volunteers in any program.

The discrepancy between the skills noted by applicants and processes of advocacy that some expected to practice underscored an area of needed training. The difference between the social skills stressed by many applicants and their focus on advocacy as one form of assistance they could provide perhaps fostered some of the difficulty they anticipated early on with the complaint process (see chapter 3). Both as applicants and as volunteers, they identified aspects of the investigative process that suggested needed intervention.

Instruction in the Complaint and Investigative Process

Contact with and development of rapport with residents are significant underpinnings of a resident advocacy program. Some volunteers indicated that they needed instruction in conducting a visit and gathering information from residents. These needs ranged from something so straightforward as "I do not know what to say to residents" to "I need to know how and what information to get from residents."

Instruction was also needed in techniques in several other instrumental activities in the investigative process. Volunteers needed techniques for observing, verifying complaints, and presenting and reporting complaints in such a way to maximize their resolution. Advocates needed to know how to report and manage complaints that might involve friends and acquaintances. As one volunteer observed, "Taking a stand on behalf of a resident when a friend or acquaintance may be implicated requires courage." Ideally, volunteer advocates would not serve in facilities where they are friends of employees, although this is often not possible in small communities. Chapter 7 shows that acting on an ideology of advocacy was especially difficult in smaller places when advocates and employees were friends.

Advocates wanted instruction in communicating to residents when their complaint was not verified, not deemed to warrant action, or otherwise not resolved. Volunteers also wanted to be prepared to handle unresponsiveness to complaints by administrators and needed to realize that failure to resolve them may lead to their own feelings of inefficacy and questions about their effectiveness.

The resignation of some volunteers was attributed to frustration with the lack of change in response to their requests on behalf of residents. At the same time, in their advice to future advocates, volunteers recommended patience, withholding judgment, and waiting a reasonable time for changes to be effected. A part of the instruction for advocates should include information about balancing these somewhat conflicting circumstances.

Not all of volunteers' needs were for training in instrumental practices; some concerned affective aspects of their work as well. Instruction was needed in managing the depressing parts of advocacy, including observing the deterioration of residents, grief, and loss. Managing losses made up a significant portion of advocates' anticipated and actual difficulties. The characteristics of recipients of care and the unmet needs of volunteers may be reasons that volunteering in nursing facilities is seldom a priority for most persons (Caro & Bass, 1995). The need for skills to manage grief, mourning, and changes in recipients of care, is, of course, not unique to this group of volunteers. Guardians of the aged, hospice workers, and other formal and informal caregivers may also need assistance in helping those who experience marked deterioration and death.

Preferences for Training and Educational Activities

Not all volunteers indicated preferences for specific training and educational activities that would facilitate their current work as advocates. In response to a structured question, however, between 26 to 38 percent of volunteers identified selected activities they believed would improve their current efforts as advocates (see chapter 10). A significant proportion of the volunteers noted several aspects of programming that would directly assist them and indirectly affect still others as they and their colleagues become more competent members of committees.

Volunteers requested written materials on understanding older persons (38 percent) and desired increased time allocated to teaching them skills and techniques that they could use as advocates (36 percent). In written materials and in other mediums of training, there should be an opportunity to address ageism, which was identified as a concern by some in committee records. Perhaps it should not be surprising that older volunteers who worked with older persons encountered ageism (Palmore, 1999).

Volunteers welcomed opportunities to meet with other advocates (29 percent) and to attend conferences and workshops on long-term care (26 percent). They wanted written materials on the practice of advocacy in long-term care settings (27 percent). Use of some of these preferred training and educational activities, which were identified in response to a structured question, suggest ways in which to address some of the needs expressed in responses to unstructured questions about difficulties and recommendations for training (see chapters 4 and 11). Some of the opportunities for education preferred by these volunteers are not limited specifically to an ombudsman program.

Correlates of In-Service Training: Suggestions for Practice

If an objective is to have more volunteers pursue advocacy as a primary orientation, in-service training especially may need to be directed toward somewhat older and less-educated volunteers regardless of age (see chapter 7).

Volunteers with primary orientations as advocates may expect to experience more hindrances and feelings of greater inequity (see chapter 6). The "costs" of advocacy should be acknowledged in training and in-service training, and strategies to address them should be presented.

Volunteers report greater efficacy as advocates when they believe that their own needs are not overlooked and when they work with peers who are more committed to their tasks. An implication for coordinators and others responsible for training is that volunteers who feel cared for experience greater feelings of mastery (see chapter 10). Training, in-service training, and contact with a coordinator are indicators of support for resident advocates.

In-service training enhanced both an orientation toward advocacy and feelings of greater efficacy. In turn, feelings of efficacy reduced worry by volunteers about their work as advocates. It may be tempting to overlook the importance of volunteers' "feelings" such as efficacy, mastery, or satisfaction to focus on more objective indicators of performance. Yet the literature suggests that efficacy and other social-psychological characteristics are related to retention and effectiveness (see chapters 9 and 10).

Supporting and Mentoring Volunteers

Volunteers with less experience believed they received less support, and they expressed greater needs for assistance than those with longer tenure as advocates (see chapter 5). Findings further indicated that the focus of assistance should be guided by the experience of volunteers in the program and not by their chronological age.

Inexperienced volunteers need to be assured of competent assistance as they learn and apply the skills of advocacy. Mentors who are experienced, capable advocates could be assigned to work with inexperienced volunteers over a sustained period of time. A number of volunteers believed they could have benefited from considerably more time to work with an experienced person on visits.

Implementing a mentoring system could build on and extend the buddy system recommended by several volunteers (see chapter 11). Through mentoring, newer volunteers may be able to obtain the support that they identified as a need (see chapters 5 and 9). The use of mentors should also strengthen the skills demonstrated in committees. Newer and experienced volunteers could work together to diminish the hindrances attributed to inadequately prepared volunteers that eventually undermine effectiveness of committees in managing complaints (see chapter 5). Inexperienced or poorly trained volunteers who try to assist one another may reduce their own feelings of efficacy as well as those of others (see chapter 9). There was a direct relationship between ratings of peers as efficacious and capable and the efficacy of other volunteers.

Efforts, of course, must be made to maximize feelings of efficacy and mastery among volunteers regardless of their recency in the program, but novices especially needed help. Feeling that their needs were recognized and taken care of was a source of support and enhanced feelings of efficacy of these advocates (see chapter 9). Duncan (1995) stressed the importance of caring for volunteers through training, follow-up, and recognition for service. Specialized training and designation as a mentor could be one form of recognition. Another form of recognition would be additional specialized training for persons holding positions such as committee chair. In turn, subsequent increased feelings of efficacy and competency of individuals should contribute to retention, to better functioning committees, and to improved care of residents.

Some Implications for Coordinators of Volunteers

This study did not focus directly on concerns of coordinators or supervisors who worked with volunteers. Nonetheless, data from the structured questionnaire indicated that volunteers generally regarded their coordinators highly. Committee records tended to show that volunteers appreciated attendance of coordinators at their meetings and opportunities to interact with coordinators. As well as providing technical assistance, coordinators seemed to be linchpins in securing training and overseeing its application by volunteers. In addition to reporting the outcomes of committee deliberations to the Office of the State Ombudsman, training, and several other administrative responsibilities, coordinators' duties may include increasing involvement of moribund committees, assisting those with high turnover, and persuading volunteers who believe they do not need further training to rethink their position.

Throughout, coordinators had a pivotal concern with training committee chairs and other volunteers. At the same time, their own needs for training and support were likely great. Almost all coordinators of volunteers worked part-time, which likely enhanced their time constraints. A national study demonstrated that nonuse of volunteers in ombudsman programs was primarily attributed to insufficient paid staff to supervise volunteers well (Schiman & Lordeman, 1989).

Some of the needs of new, inexperienced coordinators may parallel those related by novice volunteers. Volunteer applicants highlighted lack of clarity in the complaint process and unclear investigative procedures as anticipated difficulties and continued to be troubled by these problems after becoming more experienced volunteers. Less-experienced coordinators responsible for training may share similar needs for clarifying the duties of volunteers and how they may be accomplished.

Education

The consistency with which education fosters participation in volunteer tasks is well documented (Wilson, 2000). Formal education figured in the development of interest in and skills for these volunteers' activities (see chapter 3). Formal education, however, was not an important direct determinant of most of the social-psychological outcomes of volunteering in the ombudsman program (see chapter 5). For example, perceptions of effectiveness, role strain, and need for support were not associated with level of education. But both formal education and in-service training differentiated among role orientations of volunteers and were a part of the profile of an orientation toward greater advocacy (see chapter 6). Volunteers with a stronger focus on advocacy were significantly more likely to have had these educational opportunities than persons who identified with the other patterns. In turn, individuals with a primary orientation toward advocacy, rather than friendly visiting, for example, served on committees that handled significantly more complaints and obtained more resolutions. That formal education and in-service training especially differentiated an orientation toward advocacy suggests that these characteristics may interact to both promote an ideology that emphasizes arguing the cause of the resident and provide actual skills to put the ideas into practice. Of course, educational skills attained earlier also may predispose those oriented toward advocacy to apply information from in-service training more adroitly than do volunteers with other orientations.

Community Size and Advocacy

In the literature, concern has been raised about implementing advocacy programs in rural areas, with the thought that smaller communities may be less adequately served (Lee & Gray, 1992; Netting & Hinds, 1989). The sample in the present research included volunteers and facilities located in very small places, some with populations of 500 or fewer, as well as larger ones.

The current findings suggest that there may be reason to question equity in advocacy in rural and urban areas. An orientation of advocacy held by volunteers in smaller communities may be more vulnerable and rendered less effective in the presence of facility staff who are friends or acquaintances. Administrators of long-term care ombudsman programs may want to bear in mind that informal ties between volunteers and staff in smaller places may change outcomes of the investigative process.

CONCLUDING THOUGHTS

Following the close of a century marked by numerous accomplishments in high technology, some of the concerns expressed by these volunteers may seem comparatively simplistic. Yet these needs require delicate skills of observation, nurturance, negotiation, and courage that no computerized monitoring system can now provide.

References

Antonucci, T. C., A. M. Sherman, & H. Akiyama. (1996). Social networks, support, and integration. In J. E. Birren (Ed.), *Encyclopedia of gerontology*. San Diego, CA: Academic Press.

Arcus, S. (1999). The long-term care ombudsman program: A social work perspective. *Journal of Gerontological Social Work, 31,* 195–206.

Atchley, R. (1997). *Social forces and aging.* Belmont, CA: Wadsworth.

Bandura, A. (1997). *Self-efficacy: The exercise of control.* New York: W. H. Freeman.

Barney, J. (1987). Community presence in nursing homes. *The Gerontologist 27,* 367–369.

Baruch, G., & R. Barnett. (1987). Role quality and psychological well-being. In F. Crosby (Ed.), *Spouse, parent, worker.* New Haven, CT: Yale University Press.

Belsky, J. (1992). The research findings on gender issues in aging men and women. In B. Wainrib (Ed.), *Gender issues across the life cycle.* New York: Springer.

Black, B., & P. Kovacs. (1999). Age-related variation in roles performed by hospice volunteers. *Journal of Applied Gerontology, 18,* 479–497.

Bull, C. N. (1998). Aging in rural communities. *National Forum, 79,* 38–44.

Bull, C. N., & N. Levine. (1993). *The older volunteer: An annotated bibliography.* Westport, CT: Greenwood Press.

Caro, F., & S. Bass. (1995). Increasing volunteering among older people. In S. Bass (Ed.), *Older and active: How Americans over 55 are contributing to society.* New Haven, CT: Yale University Press.

Chambré, S. (1987). *Good deeds in old age: Volunteering by the new leisure class.* Lexington, MA: Lexington Books.

Cherry, R. (1991). Agents of nursing home quality of care: Ombudsmen and staff ratios revisited. *The Gerontologist, 31,* 302–308.

Clary, E., M. Snyder, & A. Stukas. (1996). Volunteers' motivations: Findings from a national survey. *Nonprofit and Voluntary Sector Quarterly, 25(4),* 485–505.

Cnaan, R., & R. Goldberg-Glen. (1991). Measuring motivation to volunteer in human services. *Journal of Applied Behavioral Science, 27,* 269–284.

Cnaan, R., F. Handy, & M. Wadsworth. (1996). Defining who is a volunteer: Conceptual and empirical considerations. *Nonprofit and Voluntary Sector Quarterly, 25,* 364–383.

Coffman, D., & M. Adamek. (1999). The contributions of wind band participation to quality of life of senior adults. *Music Therapy Perspectives, 17,* 27–31.

Coward, R. T., R. P. Duncan, & R. Uttaro. (1996). The rural nursing home industry: A national perspective. *Journal of Applied Gerontology, 15,* 153–171.

Coward, R. T., J. K. Netzer, & C. W. Peek. (1996). Obstacles to creating high-quality long-term care services for rural elders. In G. D. Rowles, J. E. Beaulieu, & W. W. Myers (Eds.), *Long-term care for the rural elderly.* New York: Springer.

Dancy, J., & M. Wynn-Dancy. (1995). The nature of caring in volunteerism within geriatric settings. *Activities, Adaptation, and Aging, 20,* 5–12.

Davey, G. C. L., M. Jubb, & C. Cameron. (1996). Catastrophic worrying as a function of changes in problem-solving confidence. *Cognitive Therapy and Research, 20,* 333–344.

Department of Health and Human Services, Office of the Inspector General. (1991). *Successful ombudsman programs.* Report No. OEI-02–90–02120. Washington DC: Department of Health and Human Services.

Duncan, M. H. (1995). Finding nursing home volunteers with staying power. *Activities, Adaptation, and Aging, 20,* 15–23.

Eden, D., & J. Kinnar. (1991). Modeling galatea: Boosting self-efficacy to increase volunteering. *Journal of Applied Psychology, 76,* 770–780.

Evans, B. (1996). Countering problem behavior with help from your ombudsman. *Activities, Adaptation, and Aging, 21(1),* 57–61.

Filinson, R. (1995). A survey of grass roots advocacy organizations for nursing home residents. *Journal of Elder Abuse and Neglect, 7,* 75–91.

Fischer, L., D. Mueller, & P. Cooper. (1991). Older volunteers: A discussion of the Minnesota Senior Study. *The Gerontologist, 31,* 183–194.

Fischer, L., and K. Schaffer. (1993). *Older volunteers: A guide to research and practice.* Newbury Park, CA: Sage.

Ginn, J., & S. Arber. (1995). Only connect: Gender relations and ageing. In S. Arber & J. Ginn (Eds.), *Connecting gender and ageing.* Buckingham, United Kingdom: Open University Press.

Goss, K. (1999). Volunteering and the long civic generation. *Nonprofit and Voluntary Sector Quarterly, 28(4),* 378–415.

Greenstein, T. (1996). Gender ideology and perceptions of the fairness of the division of household labor: Effects on marital quality. *Social Forces, 74,* 1029–1042.

Gross, D., B. Conrad, L. Fogg, & W. Wothke. (1994). A longitudinal model of maternal self-efficacy, depression, and difficult temperament during toddlerhood. *Research in Nursing and Health, 17,* 207–215.

Guterbock, T., & J. Fries. (1997). *Maintaining America's social fabric: The AARP survey of civic involvement.* Washington DC: AARP.

Harootyan, R. A. (1996). Volunteer activity by older adults. In J. E. Birren (Ed.), *Encyclopedia of Gerontology.* San Diego, CA: Academic Press.

Harrington, C., D. Zimmerman, S. Karon, J. Robinson, & P. Beutel. (2000). Nursing home staffing and its relationship to deficiencies. *Journal of Gerontology, 55,* S278–S287.

Harris-Wehling, J., J. Feasley, & C. Estes. (1995). *Real people real problems: An evaluation of the long term care ombudsman programs of the Older Americans Act.* Washington DC: Division of Health Care Services, Institute of Medicine.

Hasselkus, B. (1988). Meaning in family caregiving: Perspectives on caregiver and professional relationships. *The Gerontologist, 28,* 686–691.

Herzog, R., M. Franks, H. Markus, & D. Holmberg. (1998). Activities and well-being in older age: Effects of self-concept and educational attainment. *Psychology and Aging, 13,* 179–185.

Herzog, R., & H. Markus. (1999). The self-concept in life span and aging research. In V. Bentson & K. Schaie (Eds.), *Handbook of theories of aging.* New York: Springer.

Hooyman, N., & H. A. Kiyak. (2002). *Social gerontology: A multidisciplinary perspective* (6th ed.). Boston: Allyn and Bacon.

Huber, R., K. Borders, K. Badrak, E. Netting, & W. Nelson. (2001). National standards for the long-term care ombudsman program and a tool to assess compliance: The Huber Badrak Borders scales. *The Gerontologist, 41,* 264–271.

Huber, R., K. Borders, F. Netting, & J. Kautz. (2000). Interpreting the meaning of ombudsman data across states: The critical analyst-practitioner link. *Journal of Applied Gerontology, 19,* 3–5.

Huber, R., K. Borders, E. Netting, & W. Nelson. (2001). Data from long-term care ombudsman programs in six states: The implications of collecting resident demographics. *The Gerontologist, 41,* 61–68.

Hunt, S. (2000). *Best practices: Training programs for long term care ombudsmen.* Washington DC: National Long Term Care Ombudsman Resource Center.

Independent Sector. (1998). *America's senior volunteers.* Washington DC: Independent Sector.

Jirovec, R., & C. Hyduk. (1998). Type of volunteer experience and health among older adult volunteers. *Journal of Gerontological Social Work, 30,* 29–42.

Keith, P. (1999). *Doing good for the aged: Volunteer advocates in nursing facilities.* A final report to the AARP Andrus Foundation. Ames: Iowa State University.

Keith, P., & R. Wacker. (1994). *Older wards and their guardians.* Westport, CT: Praeger.

Kovacs, P., & B. Black. (1999). Volunteerism and older adults: Implications for social work practice. *Journal of Gerontological Social Work, 32,* 25–39.

Krout, J. A. (1994). Rural aging community-based services. In R. T. Coward, C. N. Bull, G. Kukulka, & J. M. Galliher (Eds.), *Health services for rural elders.* New York: Springer.

Lee, C., & L. Gray. (1992). Respite service to family caregivers by the senior companion program: An urban-rural comparison. *Journal of Applied Gerontology, 11,* 395–406.

Litwin, H., & A. Monk. (1984). Volunteer ombudsman burnout in long-term care services: Some causes and solutions. *Administration in Social Work, 8,* 99–110.

Litwin, H., & A. Monk. (1987). Do nursing home patient ombudsmen make a difference? *Journal of Gerontological Social Work, 11(1/2),* 95–104.

Lusky, R., H. Friedsam, & S. Ingman. (1994). *Provider attitudes towards the nursing home ombudsman program.* Denton: Center for Studies on Aging, University of North Texas.

Major, B., C. Cozzarelli, A. M. Sciacchitano, M. L. Cooper, M. Testa, & P. M. Mueller. (1990). Perceived social support, self-efficacy, and adjustment to abortion. *Journal of Personality and Social Psychology, 59,* 452–463.

Maslach, C., W. Schaufeli, & M. Leiter. (2001). Job burnout. *Annual Review of Psychology, 52,* 397–422.

Midlarsky, E., & E. Kahana. (1994). *Altruism in later life.* Thousand Oaks, CA: Sage.

Mirowsky, J., & C. Ross. (1986). Social patterns of distress. *Annual Review of Sociology*, 12, 23–45.

Monk, A., & L. Kaye. (1982a). Community representation and empowerment in long term care settings: The case of the nursing home patient ombudsman. *Journal of Sociology and Social Welfare*, 9, 122–133.

Monk, A., & L. Kaye. (1982b). The ombudsman volunteer in the nursing home: Differential role perceptions of patient representatives for the institutionalized aged. *The Gerontologist*, 22, 194–199.

Monk, A., L. Kaye, & H. Litwin. (1984). *Resolving grievances in the nursing home.* New York: Columbia University Press.

Morgan, L., & S. Kunkel. (2001). *Aging: The social context* (2nd ed.). Thousand Oaks, CA: Pine Forge Press.

Morrow-Howell, N., & A. Mui. 1989. Elderly volunteers: Reason for initiating and terminating service. *Journal of Gerontological Social Work*, 13, 21–34.

Musick, M., R. Herzog, & J. S. House. (1999). Volunteering and mortality among older adults: Findings from a national sample. *Journal of Gerontology: Social Sciences*, 54B, S173–S180. [Medline]

Nathanson, I., & E. Eggleton. (1993). Motivation versus program effect on length of service: A study of four cohorts of ombudservice volunteers. *Journal of Gerontological Social Work*, 19(3/4), 95–113.

National Center for State Long-Term Care Ombudsman Resources. (1992). *Comprehensive curriculum: A training resource for state long-term care ombudsman programs.* Washington DC: National Center for State Long-Term Care Ombudsman Resources.

Nelson, H. (1995). Long-term care volunteer roles on trial: Ombudsman effectiveness revisited. *Journal of Gerontological Social Work*, 23, 25–46.

Nelson, H., R. Huber, & K. Walter. (1995). The relationship between volunteer long-term care ombudsmen and regulatory nursing home actions. *The Gerontologist*, 35, 509–514.

Nelson, W. (2000). Injustice and conflict in nursing homes: Toward advocacy and exchange. *Journal of Aging Studies*, 14, 39–61.

Netting, F., & H. Hinds. (1984). Volunteer advocates in long-term care: Local implementation of a federal mandate. *The Gerontologist*, 24, 13–15.

Netting, F., & H. Hinds. (1989). Rural volunteer ombudsman programs. *Journal of Applied Gerontology*, 8, 419–431.

Netting, F., R. Huber, R. Paton, & J. Kautz. (1995). Elder rights and the long-term care ombudsman program. *Social Work*, 40, 351–357.

Okun, M., A. Barr, & A. Herzog. (1998). Motivation to volunteer by older adults: A test of competing measurement models. *Psychology of Aging*, 13, 608–617.

Okun, M., & N. Eisenberg. (1992). A comparison of office and adult day care center older volunteers: Social-psychological and demographic differences. *International Journal of Aging and Human Development*, 35, 219–233.

Oman, D., C. E. Thoresen, & K. McMahon. (1999). Volunteerism and mortality among the community-dwelling elderly. *Journal of Health Psychology*, 4, 301–316.

Omoto, A., & M. Snyder. (1993). Volunteers and their motivations: Theoretical issues and practical concerns. *Nonprofit Management Leadership*, 4, 157–176.

Palmore, E. (1999). *Ageism: Negative and positive.* New York: Springer.

Parker, P., & J. Kulik. (1995). Burnout, self and supervisor related job performance, and absenteeism among nurses. *Journal of Behavioral Medicine, 18,* 581–599.

Peek, C., R. Coward, G. Lee, & B. Zsembik. (1997). The influence of community context on the preferences of older adults for entering a nursing home. *The Gerontologist, 37,* 533–542.

Perry, W. (1983). The willingness of persons 60 or over to volunteer: Implications for the social services. *Journal of Gerontological Social Work, 5,* 107–118.

Rowles, G. D. (1996). Nursing homes in the rural long-term care continuum. In G. D. Rowles, J. E. Beaulieu, & W. W. Myers (Eds.), *Long-term care for the rural elderly.* New York: Springer.

Rowles, G. D., J. E. Beaulieu, & W. W. Myers. (1996). Introduction: Long-term care for the rural elderly—The legacy of the twentieth century. In G. D. Rowles, J. E. Beaulieu, & W. W. Myers (Eds.), *Long-term care for the rural elderly.* New York: Springer.

Rumsey, D. (1997). Motivational factors of older adult volunteers. *Dissertation Abstracts International Section A: Humanities and Social Sciences, 58,* 0699.

Schaufeli, W., & B. Janczur. (1994). Burnout among nurses: A Polish-Dutch comparison. *Journal of Cross Cultural Psychology, 25,* 95–113.

Scheibel, J. (1996). Recruiting the over-the-hill gang for national service. *Social Policy, 27,* 30–35.

Schiman, C., & A. Lordeman. (1989). *A study of the use of volunteers by long term care ombudsman programs: The effectiveness of recruitment, supervision, and retention.* Washington DC: The National Association of State Units on Aging, The National Center for State Long Term Care Ombudsman Resources. AOA-DHHS No. 90-ATO401.

Scott, J. P., & J. Caldwell. (1996). Needs and program strengths: Perceptions of hospice volunteers. *Hospice, 11,* 19–30.

Shaughnessy, P. W. (1994). Changing institutional long-term care to improve rural health care. In R. T. Coward, C. N. Bull, G. Kukulka, & G. M. Galliher (Eds.), *Health services for rural elders.* New York: Springer.

Singer, M. S., & T. Coffin. (1996). Cognitive and volitional determinants of job attitudes in a voluntary organization. *Journal of Social Behavior and Personality, 11,* 313–328.

Singh, D. A., & R. C. Schwab. (1998). Retention of administrators in nursing homes: What can management do? *The Gerontologist, 38,* 362–269.

Sprecher, S. (1992). How men and women expect to feel and behave in response to inequity in close relationships. *Social Psychology Quarterly, 55,* 57–69.

Stebbins, R. (1996). Volunteering: A serious leisure pursuit. *Nonprofit and Voluntary Sector Quarterly, 25,* 211–224.

Sundeen, R. (1990). Family life course status and volunteer behavior: Implications for the single parent. *Sociological Perspectives, 33,* 483–500.

Tourigny-Rivard, M., & M. Drury. (1987). The effects of a monthly psychiatric consultation in a nursing home. *The Gerontologist, 27,* 363–366.

Turner, H. B. (1992). Older volunteers: An assessment of two theories. *Educational Gerontology, 18,* 41–55.

Van Willigen, M. (1997). Social-psychological benefits of voluntary work: The impact of participation in political activism, community service work, and volunteering on individual well-being. Ph.D. diss., The Ohio State University.

Van Willigen, M. (2000). Differential benefits of volunteering across the life course. *Journal of Gerontology, 55,* S308–S318.

Van Willigen, M., & P. Drentea. (1997). Benefits of equitable relationships: The impact of sense of fairness, household division of labor, and decision-making power on social support. Association paper. *Sociological Abstracts.*

Van Yperen, N., & B. Buunk. (1990). A longitudinal study of equity and satisfaction in intimate relationships. *European Journal of Social Psychology, 20,* 287–309.

Wacker, R., K. Roberto, & L. Piper. (1998). *Community resources for older adults.* Thousand Oaks, CA: Sage.

Warburton, J., D.J. Terry, L.S. Rosenman, & M. Shapiro. (2001). Differences between older volunteers and nonvolunteers: Attitudinal, normative, and control beliefs. *Research on Aging, 23(5),* 586–605.

Wheeler, J., K. Gorey, & B. Greenblatt. (1998). The beneficial effects of volunteering for older volunteers and the people they serve: A meta-analysis. *International Journal of Aging and Human Development, 47,* 69–79.

Wilson, J. (2000). Volunteering. *Annual Review of Sociology, 26,* 215–240.

Wilson, J., & M. Musick. (1997). Who cares? Toward an integrated theory of volunteer work. *American Sociological Review, 62,* 694–713.

Young, F.W., & N. Glasgow. (1998). Voluntary social participation and health. *Research on Aging, 20,* 339–362.

Zweigenhaft, R., J. Armstrong, F. Quintis, & A. Riddick. (1996). The motivation and effectiveness of hospital volunteers. *Journal of Social Psychology, 136,* 25–34.

Index

About the Author

PAT M. KEITH is Professor of Sociology, Iowa State University.